# micro
# shelters

# micro
# shelters

## 59
**CREATIVE CABINS, TINY HOUSES, TREE HOUSES, AND OTHER SMALL STRUCTURES**

**DEREK "DEEK" DIEDRICKSEN**

Storey Publishing

The mission of Storey Publishing is to serve our customers by
publishing practical information that encourages
personal independence in harmony with the environment.

**EDITED BY** Deborah Balmuth and Hannah Fries
**TECHNICAL EDITING BY** Philip Schmidt
**ART DIRECTION AND BOOK DESIGN BY** Carolyn Eckert
**TEXT PRODUCTION BY** Michaela Jebb

**COVER PHOTOGRAPHY BY:**

© Derek Diedricksen: spine (top);

© Dustin Diedricksen: back;

© Jean-Marc and Maggie Labrosse: front
   (bottom right);

© John Polak: front (left), inside front;

ModFruGal: spine (middle);

© Nathan Rist: spine (bottom);

© Sean F. White: front (top right)

**INTERIOR PHOTOGRAPHY CREDITS** appear on
   page 256

**ILLUSTRATIONS BY:**

© Derek Diedricksen: "favorite features," 14, 54,
   102, 128, 148;

Lee Mothes: back cover (left), plan drawings
   (throughout), 164–171, 181;

© Phil Hackett: back cover (right), 7 (bottom right),
   11, 12–13, 160–161, 179, 192, 200–201, 204, 212, 222,
   232, 240, 250

**© 2015 BY DEREK DIEDRICKSEN**

Take proper safety precautions before using potentially dangerous tools and equipment or undertaking
potentially dangerous activities. Follow all applicable state and local building codes.

**STOREY PUBLISHING**
210 MASS MoCA Way
North Adams, MA 01247
www.storey.com

Printed in China by Toppan Leefung Printing Ltd.
10  9  8  7  6  5

Library of Congress Cataloging-in-Publication Data

Diedricksen, Derek.
   Microshelters : 59 creative cabins, tiny houses,
   tree houses, and other small structures /
   Derek Diedricksen.
      pages cm
   ISBN 978-1-61212-353-0 (pbk. : alk. paper)
   ISBN 978-1-61212-354-7 (ebook)  1.  Outbuildings.
   I. Title.
TH4955.D54 2015
690'.89—dc23

                                    2015009864

# Acknowledgments

This book would not have been possible without all the designers, builders, backyard tinkerers, and weekend warriors (many who became my friends along the way) who shared stories and photos of their microshelters. Please be sure to see the resource list in the back of the book to find their websites.

Thanks also goes out to my wife, Liz, for her undying encouragement and tolerance in the face of our Backyard Oompa Loompa Village of Weird Shacks, Forts, and Tiny Houses (she's a trooper! and absolutely amazing). An additional Kong-sized nod is due to my brother, Dustin, who has helped me so many times with builds and workshops around the US; to the Bendix family for all of their support over the years; and to my parents, Glenn and Sigrid Diedricksen, for such a fun and creativity-laden upbringing.

I also can't forget Steven Harrell, Kent Griswold, Michael Janzen, Lloyd Kahn, Macy Miller, Andrew Odom, Joe Everson, and Alex Pino — some very supportive friends in the industry.

And thanks to you for picking up this book.
You have exceptionally good taste — I don't care what all
the others have said about you . . .

— Deek

# CONTENTS

# WHAT'S WITH THE "TINY" OBSESSION?

**'VE BEEN ASKED** this question many times, and there's no easy answer. I just dig tiny, cozy structures. As to why, there are numerous reasons, some you might not anticipate.

Creating a microstructure involves creative thinking, outdoor activity, and problem-solving — things many people crave but often find absent from their busy (and sometimes repetitious and regimented) modern lives. And not only is it a relatively affordable pursuit, it also requires far less time and patience than building something of "ginormous" proportions. That's the beauty of very tiny projects: they're easy on both the wallet and the mind.

Their small size also makes them easy on the neighbors.

Depending on where you live you can also build many structures, including many in this book, without a permit. Heck, if you do need a permit and later get busted for building without one (not that I'm encouraging that . . .), how hard is it to relocate a diminutive backyard hut or office? Toss that sucker on the back of a truck, or haul it off-site with a flatbed, and you're good to go.

Building small requires relatively few resources, and you'll find many structures here that have been designed around, and built with, free, salvaged, and recycled materials. By taking this path you're keeping materials out of the waste stream and preventing them from clogging up landfills. You're also saving yourself a good deal of money while working unique and character-rich design elements into your home, office, or hideout. Sure, permit-wise, recycled goods may not be allowed in the construction of full-out homes, but with tinier builds and backyard hideouts that don't require town-hall paperwork, often there can be a lot more leeway. In some more rural areas you could even build a home out of recycled fast-food wrappers and bubble gum and no one would give you any guff . . . well, except the ants, perhaps.

If you're leafing through this book for ideas on building a full-time home, keep in mind that modestly sized dwellings are not only relatively cheap and quick to construct, they're also easy and inexpensive to heat, cool, maintain, furnish, and clean.

If you're a beginner builder you'll also like to know that small projects are more forgiving of mistakes . . . even big ones. I mean, how bad can it really get? If things were to go horribly and irreparably wrong, which is not likely, you could start over completely with little financial pain. But overall, planning is key. Take your time.

Finally, in a lot of cases, small spaces just work well, even if you're only looking to build a tiny backyard office that saves you from that soul-taxing commute to work or the overhead of a rented office space. Small spaces are private and intimate, and they give you a feeling of control over your domain. This is strengthened by the fact that you, as the designer and/or builder, have had to carefully consider the smallest details of placement, storage needs, and overall flow of space.

In my many travels for my work, I've been lucky enough to stay in numerous tiny houses, backyard cottages,

houseboats, and even tree houses, many of which handle these details in interesting and beautiful ways. I've enjoyed spending the night in these unusual shelters and homes and seeing how the design-minds of others work. Some ideas I've loved; others I'd personally pass on. (In this book I offer my own take on each design in a Favorite Features section.)

Consider this book a collection of ideas in creative simplicity. It's eclectic, and the works within come from a good many contributors from across the US and elsewhere. The designs represent a large and varied range in style, taste, and function. After all, who wants to see a dull-as-toast collection of all-the-same, never-daring microstructures that were seemingly plopped off an assembly line? Not I.

Welcome to a world of imaginative, out-there fun — all within the realm of "shelter," from the most basic

to the utterly brain-bending. You'll find pretty much everything: little cabins, tiny houses, "shoffices" (shed-offices), kids' forts and playhouses, homes on wheels, tree houses, guest huts, backyard retreats, garden follies, and simple shacks. My aim is to deliver as many new concepts and design approaches as possible and to offer you fresh ideas, fuel for future projects, and techniques and approaches you might not have considered. In other words, I hope this book lights a fire under your bottom.

Now get out there and *create*!

— **Derek "Deek" Diedricksen**
(from a 40-square-foot, backyard office —
not to mention many airplane terminals,
late nights in front of bad TV, and the deep woods
of Vermont by candlelight)

# MICRO

**A smaller structure . . .**

- costs less to build.
- can be built more quickly.
- can often be built out-of-pocket, without loans.
- is easier to heat and cool.
- is easier to clean, furnish, and maintain.
- can often be tackled by a novice builder.
- is easier to move.
- is less site-invasive.
- poses less to lose.
- is easier to hide, if privacy or security is what you're gunning for.
- prevents you from being able to buy junk and things you don't need (there's no room for them).
- is less likely to be over-visited by the in-laws (no space for 'em!).

- requires fewer materials and resources.
- produces less construction waste.
- affords you the luxury of handpicking your materials and lumber.
- is easier and cheaper to decorate.
- can be built without the cost and hassle of permits in many areas.
- allows you to manage, build, tweak, design, and complete the project yourself, in many cases (how many people hold those bragging rights?).
- allows you to make mistakes that are less costly and infuriating.
- is fun, in a back-to-your-childhood, small, intimate, quiet-space way.
- is cozy.
- is your own.
- *is something you can start planning now.*

# tiny houses

**1**

**PEOPLE HAVE LONG ARGUED** about what makes a house a real-deal home. Opinions on what characterizes a permanent, full-time dwelling differ by taste, of course, but also by region and culture. The homes in this section have a few essential elements: sleeping quarters, a toilet of some sort, a place to wash oneself (if not contained within, then very close by), and areas for food preparation and storage. Eat, sleep, digest — that's what it boils down to, and the dwellings here have that covered.

# MATT WOLPE'S TINY HOUSE

**Just Fine
Design/Build**

**100 square feet**

**Oakland,
California**

**M**ATT'S SELF-DESIGNED and self-built home is proof that it's possible to fit many of the regular amenities of a more standard-size home into a tiny one. It's one of my very favorite tiny dwellings on the scene and is just *loaded* with character. Wolpe, who co-heads (with partner Kevin McElroy) the design firm Just Fine Design/Build, managed to squeeze a full kitchen with a two-burner range, a greywater system, a full bed in a lofted area, a Dickinson propane stove, and more all into only 100 square feet. Though the bathroom is off-site, Matt hid an outdoor shower in the back, seeing as Oakland's climate makes it a more desirable setup than it might be elsewhere. Aside from that, the house resembles a traditional home, albeit tinier. The budget was equally tiny. Overall, Matt spent only $5,500 on his home, which is impressive, considering the look and feel he was able to achieve within. Oh yeah, it's also made with a huge amount of free, salvaged, and repurposed materials, so an extra nod goes out to Matt for that alone.

## Matt Wolpe's Floor Plan

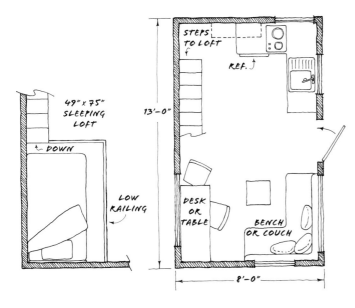

STEPS TO LOFT

REF.

49" x 75" SLEEPING LOFT

13'-0"

DOWN

LOW RAILING

DESK OR TABLE

BENCH OR COUCH

8'-0"

**favorite features**

What I like most about Matt's home is that it includes many modern conveniences without making the place seem cramped. By leaving a good deal of open living space, Matt has made his little home feel significantly bigger than it really is. Additionally, all of his hardwood furniture was hand-built, and his floors were taken from an old roller skating rink and given new life — a great conversation piece right there, never mind that this little house is just beautiful. Built-in furniture, it should be noted, is certainly something to consider in a small house or microstructure. Most standard couches, tables, ottomans, and benches don't fit easily in a space so small, so you might want to consider custom-building your own pieces instead. They can be as fancy or as rustic as you'd like, any color you desire, and, well, built exactly the way you want . . . with a little elbow grease. You'll probably save some money, and you just might have some fun, too!

Floorboards salvaged from roller-skating rink

# LITTLE YELLOW

**O** **N A VISIT OUT** to San Francisco to speak at a workshop for the Tumbleweed Tiny House Company, I luckily found time for a side jaunt to Half Moon Bay to see the micro-residence of Ella Jenkins. Ella's self-built house is a prime example of how to make a home one's own: she's taken the time to design and arrange her living space and belongings to reflect her needs, routines, and tastes. For many, building a tiny house or microstructure, for any use, is a once-in-a-lifetime DIY task. It's certainly one you'll want to be proud of. So why not build it to suit your own needs and desires?

Original plans by **Tumbleweed Tiny House Company,** altered by Ella Jenkins

**120 square feet**

**Half Moon Bay, California**

Little Yellow is based on a design from Tumbleweed Tiny House Company (their Fencl model at the time). Among her many adjustments to the original design, Ella eliminated the Dutch hip roof on the entrance end of the home to bring out the gable to the full trailer's length. This yielded extra storage space in the secondary loft and, as an added bonus, made the roof much easier to frame. Fewer cuts, angles, and figuring often result in fewer headaches.

A sleeping loft at the rear end of the house frees up living and cooking space below. This well-appointed home also features a composting toilet, a shower stall fashioned from a rather funky and fun-looking stock feed tank, and a bay window with a view (of a horse farm). There's ample space for Ella's large harp, the focal point of the main room, and a salvaged vintage school desk where she can sit and work on her handmade jewelry. She even has room left over to entertain guests, all within 120 square feet. Is it magic? Nope, just the result of a good dose of planning and knowing what one wants.

Hanging
dish rack

Manzanita
bough

Overall, Ella's Little
Yellow has a more
thoughtful and
intentional feel
than many of the
homes I've set foot
in — and there have
been many. I love
her choice of inte-
rior colors, which
are vibrant without
being overwhelm-
ing. Her combined
dish storage and
drainage rack (the
rack hangs above
the sink and drips
right into it) is an
excellent exam-
ple of thrift and
space efficiency.
Also noteworthy
is the post of her
front porch. This
thick, debarked
manzanita bough,
grabbed from the
side of a cliff, tells
the visitor from
the very start,
"You're about to
enter a pretty darn
unique home."
The manzanita
ain't lyin'.

MAIN LEVEL

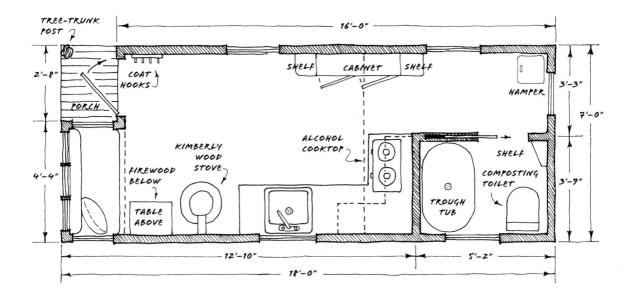

LOFT

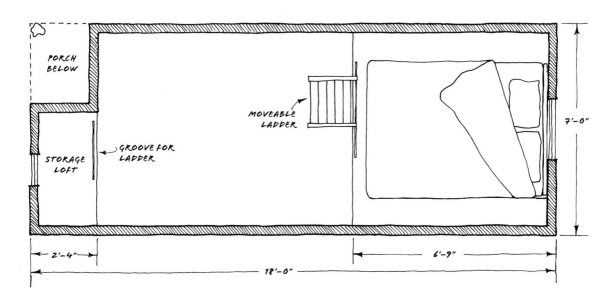

High ceiling

Plywood wall cladding

# THE 227

**Yestermorrow Design/Build School**

**227 square feet**

**Western Massachusetts**

**O**N A CAFFEINE-FUELED romp through the Berkshires and beyond, my brother, Dustin (aka "Dr. Demolition"), and I hit five unusual tiny cabins and dwellings in just two days, photographing and shooting videos of each along the way. It was our "Two Days, Three States, Five Locales, Nine Videos, and 47 Cups of Coffee" tour. Well, maybe not 47. The point is, it was a fun but tiring tour, and by the time we reached the 227, our last stop, I was in a let's-just-get-this-last-shoot-over-with state of mind. Well, as we pulled up we were greeted by Jesse, one of the owners, who gave us fresh eggs and a look at a great new barn he had just designed. Then we saw the house. We were wowed by the appearance and layout of this very sparse and modern home. My mindset was changed instantly, and I was now excited (or coffee number 47 had finally kicked in!).

At 227 square feet the house is one of the larger structures covered in this book, but it's still a far cry from the average-size home in not only the United States, where excess reigns supreme, but also worldwide. The team from the Yestermorrow Design/

Build School in Warren, Vermont, did a pretty exceptional job with the layout of this mini-home, which, I might add, is on wheels. Charred *shou sugi ban* siding (a Japanese technique of sealing the wood with a blowtorch), recycled metal light and handle fixtures, crafty storage nooks and drawers, and high ceilings all go a long way in making this a very attractive little dwelling. The bathroom, with a large, custom sliding wall/door and almost 30 square feet in size, is rather luxurious by tiny-house standards. Borrowing from nautical design, the room is a *wet bath*, in which the shower, sink, and composting toilet are all in the same open space. Slatted floors ensure drainage, as no one wants to splash their way to a toilet when duty calls.

I can't get enough of the steampunk-esque, pipe-fitting ceiling lamps of the 227. So many people overlook the simple concept of using raw-looking plywood as wall cladding. Not only can it look great, but it saves time, money, and materials, not to mention weight in cases where trailer loads are a concern. The variously textured bed drawers are good-looking and fun, in addition to providing a wealth of storage space. The polycarbonate wall panels also have a great look. These make for lightweight, easy-to-install walls with an almost space-age effect.

## 227 Floor Plan

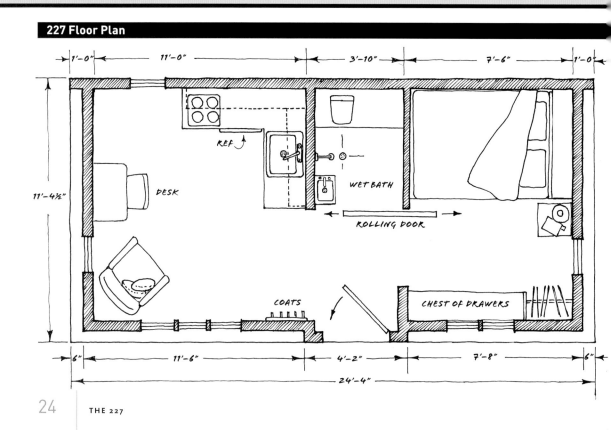

# MENDY'S SHOE BOX

**A**RGUABLY ONE OF THE HARDER-WORKING dudes in the "tiny industry," Joe Everson (plus Joe Sr., Chris Cole, and their team at Tennessee Tiny Homes) seems to have a zeal for construction and small space design that is surpassed by few. With over 15 years of building and framing experience under his belt, Joe decided sometime around 2011 to dip his toes into the world of tiny dwellings. Since then, he has built and designed numerous homes, both "groundbound" structures and travel trailers, each one very different from its predecessor.

**Tennessee Tiny Homes**

**120 square feet**

**Tennessee**

Mendy's Shoe Box, named for the client it was fashioned for, was one of Joe's early projects and shows his team's knack for interior style and design. One aspect I particularly love in Everson's work is the incorporation of fold-down decks that stow upward in a locked position for road travel. These also provide security when the owner is away for long periods of time. With Joe's creativity for finding storage in otherwise overlooked places, plus his team's ability to work in some rather fun color schemes, this tiny house company should be around for some time.

**favorite features**

**Mendy's Shoe Box has a great little entrance arrangement where a built-in couch — something you don't see as often as you might expect in tiny homes — also doubles as a daybed and storage cover, and it's conveniently positioned across from a wall-mounted TV. Joe somehow manages to stuff highly functional shower and bath combos into the smallest of spaces too.**

## Mendy's Floor Plan

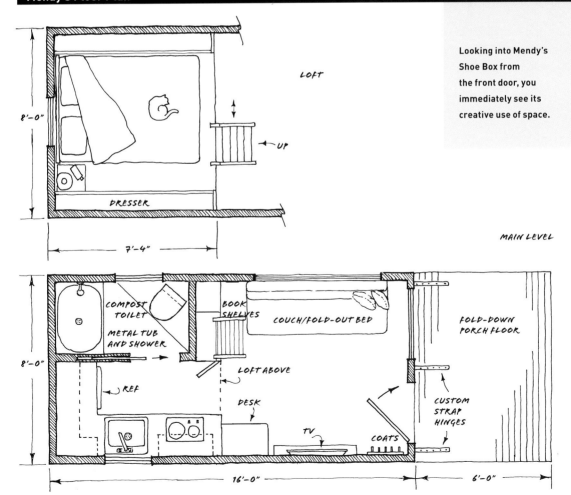

LOFT

8'-0"

DRESSER

7'-4"

← UP

Looking into Mendy's
Shoe Box from
the front door, you
immediately see its
creative use of space.

MAIN LEVEL

COMPOST
TOILET

BOOK
SHELVES

COUCH/FOLD-OUT BED

FOLD-DOWN
PORCH FLOOR

METAL TUB
AND SHOWER

8'-0"

→ REF

LOFT ABOVE

DESK

TV

COATS

CUSTOM
STRAP
HINGES

16'-0"

6'-0"

# THE TUMBLEWEED LINDEN

**Meg Stephens, Tumbleweed Tiny House Company**

**131 square feet**

**Healdsburg, California**

**T**HE TUMBLEWEED LINDEN is one of the better examples of space efficiency out there, even before factoring in the loft (which can fit a king-size mattress, with room to spare). I was lucky enough to get a tour of this place at the Sonoma County Fair as part of their Tiny Town exhibit. Upon entering, I was rather surprised at just how open this Tumbleweed felt. The Linden has the largest loft among Tumbleweed's travel trailers. It's one in a series of newer models, all with tree-related names, and is available with several different floor plans. This 20-foot-long home also boasts a second storage loft, one of the more useable kitchens I've seen in so small a home, *and* a real-deal, full-sized shower stall and composting toilet, which have been fit cunningly into the tiny bathroom. This is achieved by borrowing a sliver of space from the end of the kitchen, where one barely notices the loss — I didn't. Add in dormers, a fairly sizable "great room" at almost 7 x 9 feet, and plenty of wall space for art and shelving, and it all starts adding up to an aesthetically pleasing and highly functional microhome.

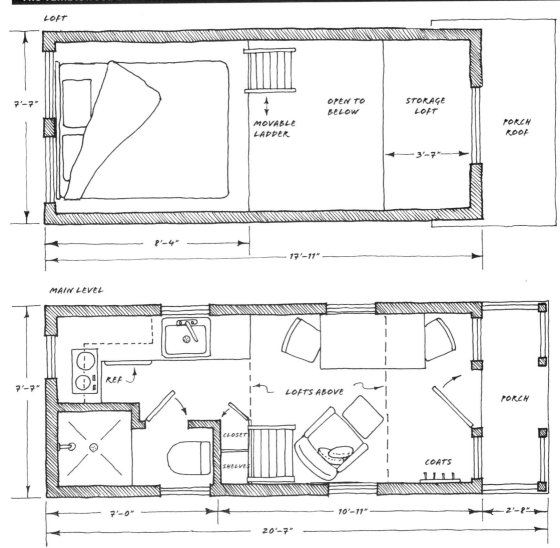

LOFT

7'-7"

MOVABLE
LADDER

OPEN TO
BELOW

STORAGE
LOFT

PORCH
ROOF

3'-7"

8'-4"

17'-11"

MAIN LEVEL

REF

7'-7"

LOFTS ABOVE

CLOSET

SHELVES

COATS

PORCH

7'-0"

10'-11"

2'-8"

20'-7"

## favorite features

The cantilevered end of the kitchen counter (just a few overhanging inches) is a nice touch in the Tumbleweed Linden, as it enables you to use it as a bar counter if you were to pull up a stool. Little details like that are what set a home apart from others. The dormer lofts and window placement also promote a nice cross-breeze, as well as ventilation in what would otherwise be a very hot loft space. The bathroom's full-shower-stall trick is so subtle most would never notice the stolen space from the kitchen. I'm also a fan of the front porch. With no railings, it becomes more open, usable, and flexible, and serves as a more gradual transition between the indoor and outdoor living spaces. The two front posts would also make for a great place to string up a temporary hammock.

Cantilevered counter extends to create a bar

# THE RUSTIC MODERN

**M**ICHAEL PAPILLO AND JENNY YEE own and operate a tiny-house bed-and-breakfast in Portland, Oregon, that they designed and built themselves. They ventured into this enterprise with a big sense of style and a very small budget. Repurposing materials for this backyard retreat not only saved them money but also set them far apart from the countless other B&Bs that dot the landscape these days.

"Sustainable design was very important to us," says Michael. The trim and shelves were created from wood nabbed from an old shed formerly on the property, and the teak flooring, otherwise very expensive, and cedar shake siding were obtained as leftovers from several high-end construction jobs. Again, the result here is not only savings but also a dose of character that gives this little oasis a look that is *so* not "off the shelf."

**Michael Papillo and Jenny Yee**

**238 square feet**

**Portland, Oregon**

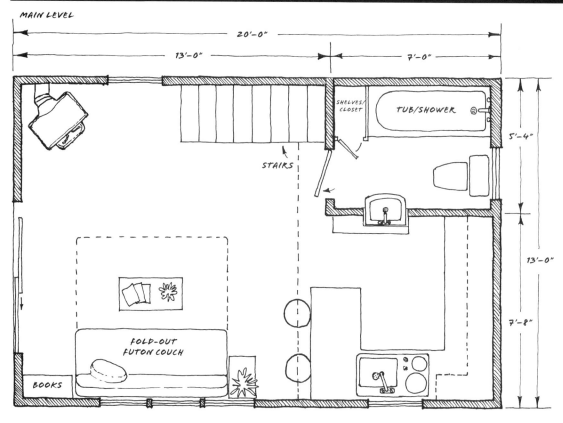

MAIN LEVEL

20'-0"

13'-0"

7'-0"

SHELVES/
CLOSET

TUB/SHOWER

5'-4"

STAIRS

13'-0"

7'-8"

FOLD-OUT
FUTON COUCH

BOOKS

LOFT

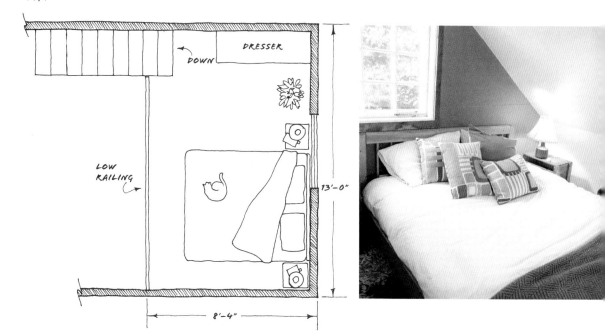

DOWN

DRESSER

LOW
RAILING

13'-0"

8'-4"

FAR LEFT: The Rustic Modern has a luxurious full bath, complete with a space-saving sink notched into the wall.

LEFT: Table made from a piece of old door

**favorite features**

In addition to the vibrant patches of color, such as the gold bathroom door, you'll find many other elements of the Rustic Modern that immediately say, "This is no boxy 'n' bland hotel room you're staying in." I really think the table made from a chunk of old door is a great idea, the orange couch adds a fun and almost punky feel to the room, and the dresser-style kitchen cabinets are unconventional yet look so at home. The loft, which houses a queen-size bed, is accessed not by a ladder but by real stairs, which many guests find much easier to use, and the rustic treads just look fantastic. It's pretty hard for me to find anything I don't like about this Portland rental.

# THE PICO-DWELLING

Steve Sauer

182 square feet

Seattle,
Washington

**T**HIS MICRO-ARCHITECTURAL BRAINCHILD of engineer Steve Sauer was born from an old storage room and speaks modernity to its very core. Steve, a bicycling enthusiast, artist, engineer, and minimalist at heart, has cleverly shoe-horned so very much into so very little. The Pico is more than just minute; it's also classy and brags a wealth of custom DIY touches. Recycled slabs of IKEA wood, for instance, have been reimagined into new tables, benches, and shelving. The custom metal work, be it railings or supports or the two elevated bed platforms, also gives this place a one-of-a-kind feel. Steps to the main sleeping loft (from the mid-level "cafe" or lounging

area) double as additional seating, and the negative voids behind them become storage space in the office nook under one of the elevated beds. It's all very well thought out, which is immediately evident when you first enter the space.

During my tour of the place Steve pointed out a feature in the bathroom: "This is perhaps the world's most expensive soap holder. It's made from laser-routed stainless steel, with inset containers from The Kitchen Store, and additional hardware welded on." You quickly understand that this is a man who knows exactly what he wants.

Creative lighting mimics daylight

**favorite features**

The Pico's layering, all within a space only 10 feet 4 inches in height, is pretty ingenious. Steve knew enough to allocate full-height spaces in select circumstances — his upright desk space beneath his bed, for instance — and when to negotiate less space and to layer certain living quarters. The latter is illustrated in a TV-viewing nook that challenges the notion that you need a lofty space to sit and watch television.

The fold-down dining room table, almost accordion-like, can hold up to six place settings and fits within a kitchen and living room space that never seems to feel cramped.

Fold-out dining table

## Pico Floor Plan

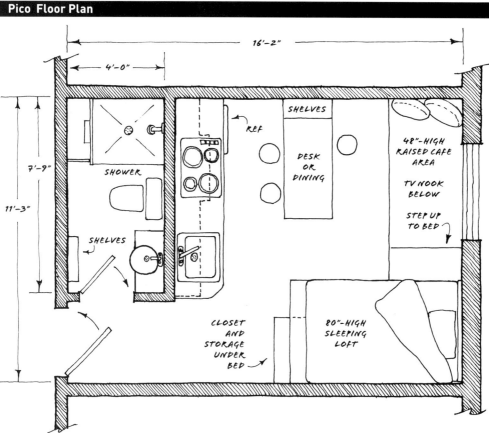

16'-2"

4'-0"

7'-9"

11'-3"

SHOWER

SHELVES

REF

SHELVES

DESK OR DINING

48"-HIGH RAISED CAFE AREA

TV NOOK BELOW

STEP UP TO BED

CLOSET AND STORAGE UNDER BED

80"-HIGH SLEEPING LOFT

# CHRIS HAYNES'S HUMBLE HOME

**Tumbleweed Tiny House Company**

**262 square feet**

**Royalston, Massachusetts**

**S**TILL QUITE SMALL IN ITS FOOTPRINT of 262 square feet, Chris Haynes's tiny house was based on a set of Bodega plans from California's Tumbleweed Tiny House Company and underwent quite a bit of tweaking to suit Chris's tastes and conform to local codes. While many of the microstructures in this book exist in an off-the-radar, don't-ask-don't-tell manner (which is why some of the locales aren't ultra-specific), Chris's place is 100 percent legal — fully permitted, fully inspected, and fully fantastic. While the sleep loft offers an additional 64 square feet of living, not to mention a good deal of storage in the eaves, it's the cathedral ceiling, only interrupted by the long run of a

Recessed cabinets

woodstove flue, that makes this home feel larger than it is. Yes, its main room is only a little over 150 square feet, but it has an impressive height of close to 15 feet. Hoops, anyone?

Chris's house is also off-grid and solar and boasts a TV entertainment system with a 50-inch projection (onto his living room's white wall) that runs on a mere, almost unheard-of 18 watts. This system, a combination of a Roku Box and a Brookstone mini projector, works very well.

Like the majority of the homes in this book, I had a chance to see Chris's firsthand, and I especially loved his rustic screened-in porch. This long, thin room overlooking a swamp provides a second sleep space in warmer weather. Come the colder months Chris has little to worry about, as the walls of his cozy little home are superinsulated, both inside the stud cavities and on the exterior. The house could almost be heated with a birthday cake.

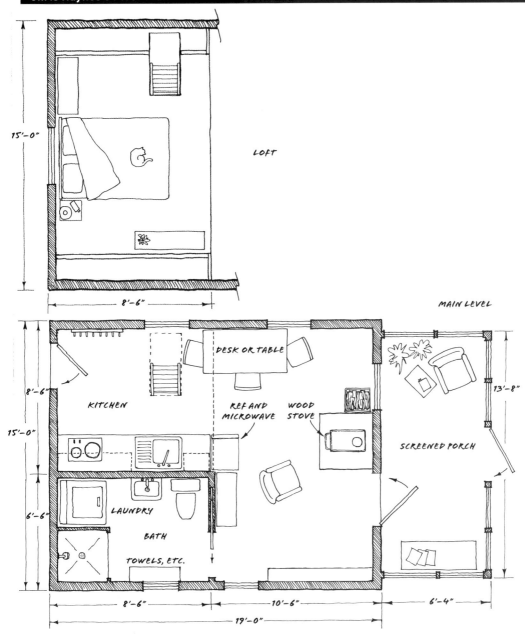

15'-0"

LOFT

8'-6"

MAIN LEVEL

8'-6"

15'-0"

6'-6"

KITCHEN

DESK OR TABLE

REF AND
MICROWAVE

WOOD
STOVE

SCREENED PORCH

13'-8"

LAUNDRY

BATH

TOWELS, ETC.

8'-6"

10'-6"

6'-4"

19'-0"

**favorite
features**

**Chris Haynes's kitchen cabinets are semi-genius in that they appear
to have little depth or storage room to them on first glance,
but once you open them, you realize that Chris has recessed them
into the wall-stud cavities. He gets the same effect with a
hollowed-out spot for his medicine cabinet in the bathroom.**

Hal's Garage Door
Murphy Bed as
seen through the
front door

# HAL'S UBER-FUNKY MICRO GUESTHOUSE

Hal Colombo

68 square feet

Seattle,
Washington

**H**AL COLOMBO, TINKERER BY DAY, musician by night, is the purveyor of one of the more unique B&Bs I've ever stayed in — and I've stayed in some *very* unusual places. How does ole Hal manage to squeeze everything you need for a cozy night's stay into an inn of Lilliputian proportions? Well, the man has quite a few tricks up his sleeve. The bathtub (yes, there's a full bathtub), for example, is set into the floor of the room and accessed by a large wooden hatch. Other creative uses of space include his phone-booth-like wet bath (a shower and toilet stall in one) and his tiered storage and counter area that doubles as steps leading up to both a sleeping loft and a sitting area on a living "green roof." Most impressive, though, is his ingenious repurposing of an automatic garage-door track and motor, which, at the push of a button, lowers the queen-sized, padded sleeping platform on the wall from a vertical to a horizontal position. It's possibly the world's first Garage Door Murphy Bed. Hal, go patent that thing!

Bathtub hatch

Green roof

Hal's Uber-Funky Micro Guesthouse just oozes charm and clever quirkiness. I love Hal's space-saving "van-ity" mirror in the bath-room (an old side-view mirror from a van), his vintage Smith Corona type-writer guest log, and the pipe-railed loft with a view of the city. Hal's main home is just as bizarre, complete with a manhole cover in the floor that connects to his workshop below, a dizzying display of vintage kitsch and odd collectibles, light-up stairs, and, to top it all off, a secret bookcase entrance to his bathroom. Batman would be proud.

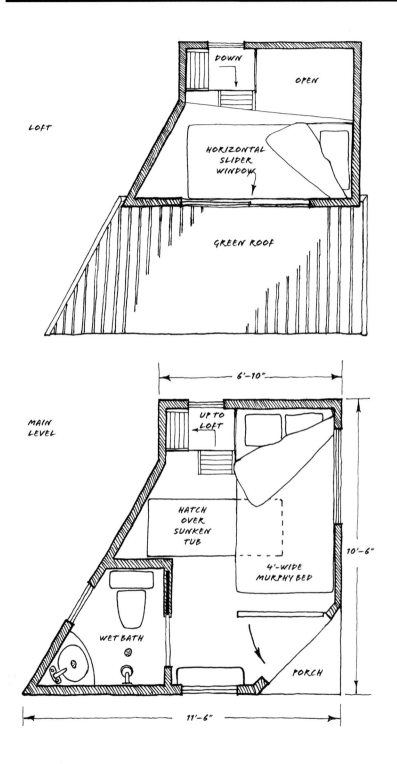

LOFT

DOWN

OPEN

HORIZONTAL SLIDER WINDOW

GREEN ROOF

MAIN LEVEL

6'-10"

UP TO LOFT

HATCH OVER SUNKEN TUB

4'-WIDE MURPHY BED

WET BATH

PORCH

10'-6"

11'-6"

# THE LUNA BLEU

**Hobbitat/Blue Moon Rising**

**300 square feet**

**Deep Creek Lake, Maryland**

**L**AUNCHED AS AN ecotourism retreat in 2013, Blue Moon Rising and its eclectic collection of rental cabins has quickly grabbed attention in the tiny-living scene due to the eye-catching design work of hired gun Bill Thomas, founder of the company Hobbitat. Lisa M. Jan, the head of Blue Moon Rising, envisioned "a built environment that preserves the existing surroundings" while integrating vacation rentals with educational courses on sustainability. One cornerstone concept of Blue Moon Rising is that nothing goes to waste, and they certainly walk the walk when it comes to choosing to team up with Bill. These lovely little lodges, wild in name (the Funkomatic 513, for instance), vary in size and style, but all of them dance in the microhome range and are shining and inspiring examples of what custom owner-built and -designed dwellings can look like. This gaggle of cabins did not fall off the assembly line of some colossal cabin kit company, that's for sure.

Lamps made from oil cans

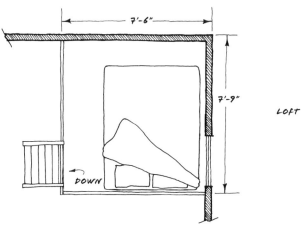

7'-6"

7'-9"

LOFT

DOWN

MAIN LEVEL

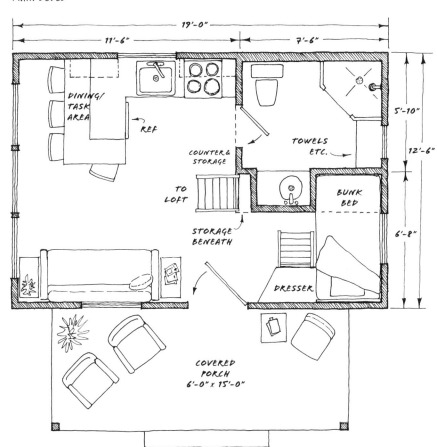

19'-0"

11'-6"

7'-6"

DINING/
TASK
AREA

REF

COUNTER &
STORAGE

TOWELS
ETC.

5'-10"

12'-6"

TO
LOFT

BUNK
BED

6'-8"

STORAGE
BENEATH

DRESSER

COVERED
PORCH
6'-0" x 15'-0"

**favorite features**

I love the recycled, distressed wood in the Luna Bleu. I also love that the Thomas-Jan team opted for both a cozy little sleep loft for the more aerially daring of over-nighters and the bunk bed nook down below. The oil can ceiling lights are also a fun, simple, homemade touch. Little details like this go a long way.

# THE MATCHBOX

Jay Austin

160 square feet

Washington, D.C.

**M**EET JAY AUSTIN, small in stature but big in style when it comes to his very unique tiny house located at the Boneyard Studios compound in Washington, D.C. Parked on a triangular sliver of land with two other tiny houses (those of Lee Pera and Brian Levy) and overlooking a local graveyard (hence the name) dotted with magnificent oak trees, Jay's boxy home stands very modern by comparison to its city surroundings. Inside, however, he has deftly joined modern and rustic accents in a very successful way. Clay-based walls, a welded steel loft, a countertop covered with real-deal moss, and a large collection of magnetic spice jars and chrome containers are just some of the usually opposing but now harmoniously cohabitating items you'll find. Jay makes it work, and he's employed a few other clever tricks around his small house too. For instance, he keeps his stowable, steel loft ladder from slipping by using strong rare-earth magnets to lock the ladder against the loft edge.

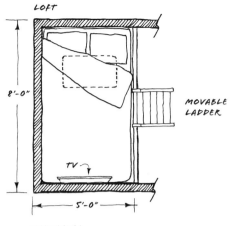

LOFT

8'-0"

MOVABLE LADDER

TV

5'-0"

Magnetic spice jars

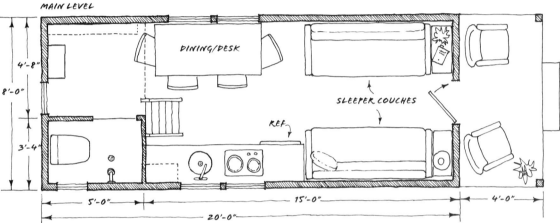

MAIN LEVEL

DINING/DESK

SLEEPER COUCHES

REF

4'-8"

8'-0"

3'-4"

5'-0"

15'-0"

4'-0"

20'-0"

## favorite features

Jay's Matchbox is one of the coziest and most appealing homes I've set foot in. It's small but feels spacious and has plenty of windows, but not so many that you feel exposed or solar-cooked. His thin steel loft saves about 2 to 3 inches of headroom that the bulk of 2x6s would have otherwise taken up, and his bathroom walls, which are not load-bearing, are mere ¾-inch wood slabs, saving 3 inches or more in horizontal space compared to 2x4 wall framing. It's a simple trick, but every inch counts. The only thing I might change (which I hear might be Jay's intent already) would be to add some sort of overhang above his front door to make the face of the home feel less two-dimensional and to serve as a dry place to fumble for keys in a rainstorm.

# THE V HOUSE

Nelson Tiny
Houses

87 square feet
(not including the
bathhouse)

British Columbia,
Canada

**T**HE V HOUSE, OR VERSATILE HOUSE, is one of Nelson Tiny Houses' signature designs. Seth Reidy and Tobias Gray build their tiny houses to suit the needs of the client — in this case, a simple but comfortable living space for one or two people. After moving this little gem into position with a crane, Seth and Tobias built a large wraparound deck and an accompanying tiny bathhouse, which features a classic claw-foot bathtub and doubles as a space for privacy and meditation. In the near future, a folding lid will be installed over the bathtub to turn it into a comfy couch when not in use for bathing. Versatile, indeed.

This particular V House is 8 feet wide and 12½ feet long and has plenty of storage, including a *cold box* (storage vented to the outdoors) recessed into the floor. It also features a bucket composting-toilet system, concrete countertops, and reclaimed solid-fir trim. All of Seth and Tobias's houses incorporate reused and reclaimed materials. The roof of this V House is even made of old road signs.

Roof made of
road signs

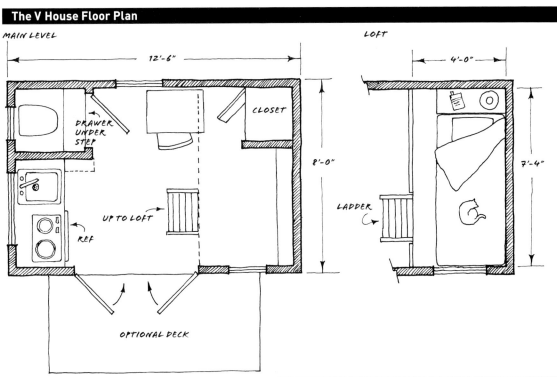

MAIN LEVEL

12'-6"

DRAWER UNDER STEP

CLOSET

8'-0"

REF

UP TO LOFT

OPTIONAL DECK

LOFT

4'-0"

7'-4"

LADDER

## favorite features

What's not to like? The V House has lean lines, a secret storage compartment or two, and, while the bathhouse is a separate building, it's only a mere four steps away. I'm also a fan of the bold, natural window trim and the shallow kitchen shelves. While they offer less storage depth, shallow shelves prevent you from having to reach over items, reshuffle things, and risk knocking the cans and glasses at the front just to get to one item stuck at the very back of a cupboard. Open and visible storage also forces you to maintain necessary minimalism and not overbuy, overstock, or overshelve unnecessary items.

Hidden storage under floor

Shallow shelves

# THE GIANT JOURNEY HOME

**Tumbleweed Tiny House Company, with alterations by Guillaume Dutilh and Jenna Spesard**

**135 square feet, plus loft**

**California**

**I**N TERMS OF STYLE, interior flow, and decor, the tiny house on wheels that is home to Guillaume Dutilh and Jenna Spesard would easily rank as one of the best I've seen. Perched on a 20-foot trailer, their dwelling-on-the-go (they've towed it around the entire US and much of Canada, blogging about their journey) is only 135 square feet, but with several space-saving and visually appealing tactics, they make it feel like you're walking into more.

This home's shiplap siding was reclaimed from a 75-year-old barn in Wisconsin, complete with buckshot scars, and the unique circular storage loft window was trimmed from a solid stump of alligator juniper.

LOFT

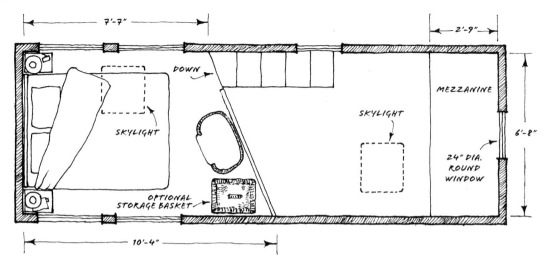

MAIN LEVEL

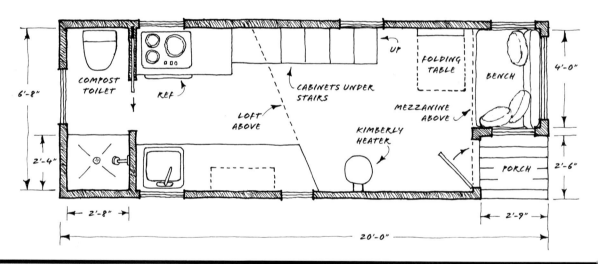

---

**favorite features**

The Giant Journey's interior layout features an affordable and appealing solution to one of the frequent concerns in the tiny house scene: "But I don't really want to climb up and down a ladder to access my bed!" Well, with a few repurposed furniture items, some salvaged crates, and even a small keg, this pair was able to build a homemade version of what the Japanese call tansu steps. The stairs are hollow, providing storage beneath, so almost no space is wasted. In addition, the initial step has been set at a height such that it can double — make that triple — as a seat. Other space savers in Guillaume and Jenna's home include magnetic cutlery storage, burlap counter curtains with storage pockets, dormers for increased loft space, a drop-down table that doubles as a chalkboard, and even basket-style seating that can be moved around into different configurations for lounging or for dinner guests.

Steps and storage in one

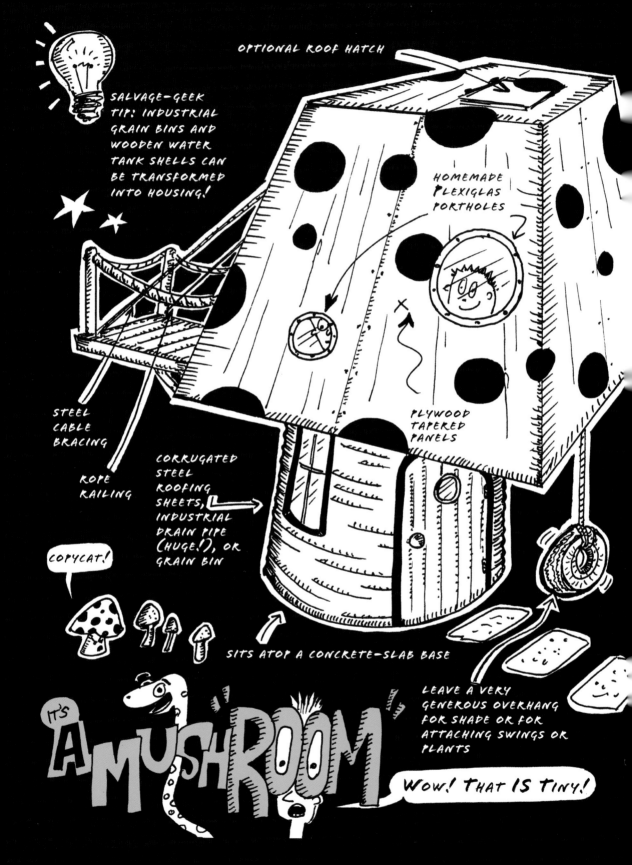

# BACKYARD CABINS, camps & hide-aways

**2**

**WHILE SOME DWELLINGS,** like those in the previous section, are geared toward extended or full-time use and are equipped to handle long stays, there are plenty of people who dig tiny spaces but might not be willing or able to live in something so, well, microscopic. For these folks — whether they are attracted to the affordability of microshelters or just to the idea of scaling down and getting away from it all — a cabin, vacation cottage, or mere backyard office just might be the fix they're looking for. So here goes: a healthy handful of camp eclecticism for you to pull ideas from.

# THE OWL HOUSE

**W**ERE I FORCED TO PICK a handful of more memorable tiny spaces, ones that just wowed the pants off me in look and approach, this would be one of them. At once whimsical, entrancing, rustic, and soothing, it employs some of the more "out there" build and decor approaches I've seen, all in a very pleasing and effective way. The Owl House is habitable art, plain and simple. From its mortared wine-bottle walls to its multihued, planked sheathing, it comes off as charming and daring. Designed and built by Madrid-based artist Leonardo Alverez Pinel, the Owl House has played host to many guests from around the world as a rental. This is no surprise — in addition to it being a marvelous piece of "living art," it sits beside a breathtaking coastal view, surrounded by miles of beach trails. Owner Tracy Lewis is just as remarkable: she's a Paralympian as well as an artist who uses recycled and found materials in her compositions and in her own home studio, which is located adjacent to the Owl House.

Leonardo Alverez Pinel

120 square feet

United Kingdom

**favorite features**

**The Owl House is stunning in its array of multihued recycled timbers, funky homemade windows, and overall vibe. The mortared bottle-end walls are a great touch, enabling light to pass through them in many colors and patterns. While the feather decor and giant eye of a window give this guesthouse its owlish motif, it's the giant "windshield" that opens it up to so much natural light and brings the interior's materials to life.**

# THE TRANSFORMING
# A-FRAME

**Deek Diedricksen,
David and Jeanie
Stiles**

**80 square feet**

**Collierville,
Tennessee**

**I** **'VE LONG BEEN** an
A-frame addict, and,
while I understand their
head-bumping shortcomings and
the challenges of pushing vertical
furniture against slanting walls,
I still can't help but love the look
and simple nature of these classic
dwellings.

This project was a team-up with
David and Jeanie Stiles, an author/
architect duo I have long admired,
resulting in a plan set that has sold
rather well online. The aims of the
project were simplicity and affordability, two things I had felt were
being driven out of the tiny housing
and vacation cabin scene. Could we

come up with a tiny cabin that slept two, had a mini storage loft with the potential to sleep one more, and a kitchenette — all in a structure that could be built for under $1,200? Yup, we could . . . and did.

Running short on time as winter descended, I found that a good many other projects on my plate were getting in the way of my actually building this design. So for the first time ever I called on a friend, Joe Everson, to tackle the actual construction. Joe heads up Tennessee Tiny Homes near Memphis, and he and his crew did a great job. They managed to bring to life all the design facets I was gunning for: two beds that double as storage, an abundance of shelving (much of it doubling as the cabin's horizontal structural elements), good ventilation and natural light (by means of a large hatch in the loft), and even a polycarbonate wall that

## favorite features

Of course I like most of what's going on with the Transforming A-Frame, since, well, I designed it. I would have liked to add a tiny bathroom or wet bath, but I also wanted to keep it very small, quick to build, and under a certain budget. I wrestled with the idea for a while but then figured that since it was supposed to be only a weekend cabin, a separate facility or outhouse would do. The flip-up porch could later be permanently framed open and made into a bathroom of sorts too. I also tried to design this A-frame in factors of two or eight feet so that anyone building it would be faced with very little wasted stock-length lumber. Additionally, I was pleased with how the loft became a means of sleeping a third person if the need arose. I won't call it spacious, but it's bigger than I expected and easily fits my 6-foot, 4-inch frame.

Translucent wall flips up to make porch roof

Beds double as storage

Loft adds sleeping space

lifts open, drops a set of legs, and becomes an open-air porch. With the wall open, you can unfurl mosquito screens for protection. This porch adds ventilation in hot weather and increases the A-frame's useable space by almost 30 square feet. Better yet, when closed, the white, translucent Tuftex wall brings in some great diffused light while maintaining privacy. At night, when lit up, the Transforming A-Frame becomes an ethereal lantern in the woods.

# JIM'S STREAMSIDE RETREAT

"**P**ULL TO THE SIDE** of the road about a half mile past North Balsam Lane. Hike until you find the waterfall on the uphill side of the road, and then, after crossing a bridge, continue along the stream until you find an old campfire ring. The cabin is a few hundred feet above that point." Those were, more or less, the directions I was given when I set out to photograph this cabin, a self-designed retreat where musician Jim Matus can gather his thoughts and focus on his songwriting. As hard as it was to find this little haven in the woods, it was a trip well worth it.

**Jim Matus**

**80 square feet**

**Conway,
Massachusetts**

Jim's cabin is a mere 8 feet deep and 10 feet wide with a single-pitch roof. It's one of the more basic cabins in this book, but also exists as proof that a cabin doesn't have to cost half a kazillion dollars and be architecturally drafted by H. R. Richinbank and Associates in order to function wonderfully while looking good. Sometimes less is more. While Jim's cabin is furnished only with a castoff coffee table, a daybed platform made from a recycled door, and the smallest of cooking and storage setups, it works for the intended occupant and should serve its owner well for years to come.

Speaking of the merits of small structures, this cabin demonstrated a case of unintended semi-portability. Apparently, it was situated too close to a stream for setback standards, and a random hiker decided to blow the whistle. The town's zoning board asked Jim to move the entire shelter almost 200 feet away, which he did, piece by piece.

Deck made from fence panel

# THE ROCK BOTTOM

**I DESIGNED THIS LITTLE CABIN** on the fly for a communal build workshop I held deep in the woods of northern Vermont. It's off the grid and has as its only lighting a Coleman lantern and other candle and oil lamps. Because half of the roof is clear Tuftex polycarbonate, when the sun goes down this micro-structure takes on a lanternlike appearance from a distance.

This 8 x 8-foot cabin is meant to be a simple, bare-bones, seasonal retreat in the woods, as well as a backwoods library of sorts. During future work-shops, a pair of attendees could stay there and enjoy the sweeping view of the woods through its many windows. We dubbed it the Rock Bottom because it was built on the most meager of budgets, it happens to be downhill from our main camp cabin, and it sits next to a very large

Deek Diedricksen

64 square feet

Derby, Vermont

boulder, a giant glacial erratic that seems to stand as the cabin's long-lost prehistoric relative.

All in all, the Rock Bottom cost a mere $300 to build, with many of its materials scavenged for free or acquired secondhand. The window in the door is a Pet Peek dome, designed to give pets a view through solid fencing, and it adds a little character to the front of the cabin. The multicolor chair inside also is made from what many would consider trash: barn boards and pallet wood. The front deck was yet another freebie. It's actually a thick fence panel that Goodridge Lumber in Albany, Vermont was tossing out. After I reinforced it from below with more free lumber, it was transformed into a nice spot where I could survey the landscape with a cold beverage while tending the nearby campfire.

**favorite features**

What I particularly like about the Rock Bottom is its simplicity. It's basically an easy-to-build A-frame that's been lifted onto short knee walls to create a little more space inside. The deck is proof that if you keep your eyes peeled and are willing to wait a little bit or think outside the box, the solution might be right under your nose. Better yet, that solution just might be a free one. The low windows come with the risk of being kicked out, but when you're stretched out in a sleeping bag, they offer a unique ground view of the forest floor and the landscape downhill.

# THE WRITER'S HAVEN

**I**'VE OFTEN BEEN ASKED in interviews, "Deek, of all the cabins and designs you've seen, which ones have been your all-time favorites?" Well, the Writer's Haven from the Vermont-based Jamaica Cottage Shop would certainly rank right up there. This 12 x 14-foot cabin, complete with a rather unusual triangular, single-posted porch, is both aesthetically pleasing and an effectively planned little getaway. It's got it all: ample space (while not eating up too much land), several windows, and a lofty ceiling. Plus, the Jamaica Cottage Shop builds most of its cabins, cottages, and sheds with a timber-frame approach, so should an elephant or three decide to sit on your roof, or have a dance-off on it, you'll most likely be fine.

Jamaica Cottage Shop

132 square feet

South Londonderry, Vermont

These things are overbuilt. But I'm sure Domenic Mangano, head honcho of the Jamaica Cottage Shop, hasn't gotten any complaints about that. Like I said, I'm a big fan of the streetside-appeal factor of the Writer's Haven. It's a good-looking little cabin that could easily be insulated and heated and put to many uses. A built-in deck doesn't hurt either. The deck *is* tiny, but extending it, if you wished, would be beyond simple. I envision the Writer's Haven perched by a tiny stream deep in the woods, harboring a little woodstove, a multicolored braided rug, an abundance of books and sketch pads, a bottle of good wine, perhaps, and the time to enjoy them all. That little front porch is just begging for a hanging chair, too, which could be unhooked to free up space that might otherwise be overwhelmed by a conventional deck chair.

Adding a loft to any cabin is an age-old technique to maximize the use of vertical space, whether for storage, sleeping space, or a reading nook.

# DIANNE AND BILL'S PLACE

**Dianne and
Bill McCoy**

**108 square feet**

**Ontario, Canada**

**I** **LOVE HEARING** land-discovery and cabin-building stories, even when I know I'll never get to visit. Dianne, a reader of my blog, contacted me with a wealth of photos and enthusiasm for their little cabin.

While visiting their daughter near Ottawa, Dianne and her husband, Bill, decided to check out a four-acre piece of property on a small creek, surrounded by a large wetland and a few farms. They had long been wanting "waterfront" property they could afford, and before they knew it the deal was sealed. Since they

already lived in a large log home they'd designed and built themselves, they opted for another log building, this time using squared timbers sourced from a local lumber mill. The original plan was for a 14 x 20-foot cabin, but it was difficult to get a building permit as there were so many restrictions. Finally, they decided on a building of 108 square feet, the maximum allowed in Ontario without a building permit. They chose dimensions of 9 x 12 feet, with an 8 x 9-foot sleeping loft cantilevered over the front of the cabin to create a covered porch and additional interior space.

and hand-washing station outside. Cooking is done outdoors on a propane camp stove. They haul in their water, and they heat with a kerosene radiant heater rather than a woodstove. "The reason," says Dianne, "is because we did not want woodsmoke to be visible in order to protect our privacy. It's for the same reason that we used green steel on the roof; it blends in with the pine, spruce, and cedar trees that surround the cabin." They'll also leave the logs to weather gray, "which will further help us blend in with the landscape." This sturdy cabin will be there for many years to come, and Dianne and Bill plan to pass it on to family someday.

The cabin has a skylight and five windows to allow for lots of natural light. There's no electricity, but Dianne and Bill hope to eventually install two small solar panels to run some lights. They also built a large outhouse with a solar shower

**favorite features**

**Dianne and Bill's cantilevered loft is a clever and often-used trick: build the base to abide by code restrictions, but then make up for the compromise in the loft, which often isn't considered useable or "habitable" space by the authorities. Blending into one's surroundings is another good idea, especially when use of the cabin is intermittent. This reduces the chance of break-ins, vandalism, and theft. Why advertise that an unattended cabin is lying there in the woods when taking only a few simple steps can reduce its visibility?**

# THE ROCK SHED

**O**NE OF THE LOCALS near my Vermont camp has a trailer that my brother, Dustin, and I have long referred to as "the chameleon." This house looks like an absolute heap of garbage from the exterior, while inside, although not exactly Xanadu, it comes off as very nice by comparison. The Rock Shed works with the same concept — ugly as sin on the outside and, well, quite unexpectedly pleasant on the in. It was also rehabbed, paint and all, for only about $400, including many of the homemade art and furniture pieces. Pallet wood, a wild array of spray paint, and roadside finds were all my friends on this constructive jaunt. The drum

**Deek Diedricksen**

**120 square feet**

**Stoughton, Massachusetts**

set, a Manhattan kit from Peace, is also a space-saver, as it takes up only 3 square feet or so. (Yes, it is possible to fit a playable, great-sounding drum set in even the tiniest of spaces!) The Rock Shed, all in all, is 10 feet wide and 12 feet deep. This is the maximum size I can build in my little Massachusetts town without needing a permit.

Skylight creates sense of spaciousness

**favorite features**

The key to this shed transformation was the 4 x 4-foot skylight we installed. This relatively large window brings a lot of natural light into the Rock Shed, creating a more spacious feeling and cheerful environment within, all for so little in cash and time. The skylight is the very first thing people notice, giving them a great view of the tree boughs above. Cost: $25 on Craigslist. I should also add that I don't usually paint things all white, but lighter colors do work well for small spaces. Truth be told, I also had access to some really inexpensive white paint. I often preach on the challenges and fun of letting the materials dictate the build, and in this case I went so far as to let nearly free paint (and my thinning wallet) guide the vibe. If you're looking to save money and make use of leftover paints, don't be afraid to mix them all together before they go to waste. You just might wind up with an extraordinary color — or, if you're not careful, some sludgy, murky brown.

# THE VISION HUT
# AT ANCIENT OAKS

Bruce Damer

110 square feet

Bay Area,
Northern
California

**T** **HE 110-SQUARE-FOOT** Vision Hut was built in 2008 by Bruce Damer and friends as a place to finish writing his PhD thesis as well as a place to meditate, practice yoga, compose music, host sleepovers, and view sunsets and the night sky from the wraparound deck.

It's part of a larger complex that includes an art bus and an octagonal stage, so funkiness already seems to be the norm at this spread. The hut looks out over a redwood valley in the Santa Cruz Mountains of Northern California. Pure Heaven, and just what the doctor ordered — literally.

**favorite features**

While I'm a fan of art-laden walls (sometimes even when they're at borderline-hoarder extremes), there's no denying the appeal of the unadorned natural wood of the Vision Hut, not to mention its great use of a small deck to extend the outdoor living space (something I always recommend, unless you live in Siberia), and that attention-grabbing, view-framing circular window. The locale doesn't hurt either! Well played, Dr. D., well played . . .

Deek Diedricksen

42 square feet

Canton,
Massachusetts

# THE RELAX SHACK

**S**INCE 2009 I've run the blog Relaxshacks.com, focused on tiny dwellings, outbuildings, and woodland-escape huts and offices. In the past, people often referred to my designs as "relax shacks," even though I'd never given a project that name. Eventually I figured it was time to use the name for real.

The idea here was to build something large enough for several uses: a backyard office, reading room, yoga studio, kid's fort, storage shed, guest sleeper, nap nook, hobby space, even a greenhouse. I also wanted to ensure that this structure was tiny enough to circumvent codes and permitting in most areas, and to be relocated without too much effort should the need arise. The result is a panelized room that's 6 feet 6 inches square. Why that and not the full run of an 8-foot board? Well, I've built a few straight 8 x 8 cabins, and that extra 18 inches, while useful, just somehow makes

The Relax Shack's windows were discovered at a town dump, the floor is made of recycled metal pool siding, and the "Wild Wall" is made of colorful scrap wood and signs.

them feel overly boxy and cumbersome instead of cute or humble. Also, the lumber I had on hand was limited in length, so this smaller dimension worked to my advantage while still being long enough to let most people stretch out for a snooze, should one decide to add in a little daybed or couch, which I later did. It's not a house, but it can make for a great little vacation cabin or guest bunkhouse for short stays, and its petite nature allows it to be plunked down on the tightest of city lots.

A tiny escape pod in the city? That could be pretty darn cool. Even cooler, you could crane this rustic yet wild-looking snooze cube up onto the rooftop of an apartment complex, or into a tree!

The Relax Shack achieved its goal of being a simple cabin in many ways: simple to build, simple to move, simple to afford, and simple to situate. I'm also a fan of the front wall of windows, another case where the materials dictated the design. Those four double-paned window sashes were freebies I found at the town dump while on vacation in China, Maine. Better yet, I was able to sell many other windows I found for $30 a pop and funneled that money into materials I couldn't find for free. The blue faux-plank flooring, by the way, is made from the recycled metal sides of an old aboveground pool that belonged to my neighbor ("crazy man" Paul LaCivita, from my YouTube series).

Not easily missed is the rear wall I've dubbed the Wild Wall. Built at a workshop, the wall was a group effort to find creative ways to use up my long-standing stock of scrap boards and found materials. The result is a tiled array of funky, multicolored, and variously textured planks, and even a few scrap wooden signs I had saved from various festivals. Look closely and you might see the remnants of a sign from New York City's Maker Faire in 2010, a display plaque from a Walden Woods build I did, a chunk of polycarbonate roofing, the oak bottoms of salvaged dressers, and even a few cartoonish images that the workshop attendees doodled in marker. In such a tiny, and initially plain-looking, cabin there's a good deal to look at, and almost all of it was crafted from nothing.

# THE MINER'S SHELTER

**Dave Frazee**

**45 square feet (plus 100 square feet exterior)**

**Taliesin West in Scottsdale, Arizona**

**T**HE MINER'S SHELTER is a desert dwelling built and designed by Dave Frazee, a student at Taliesin, the Frank Lloyd Wright School of Architecture. Both the concept and title were inspired by the architectural ruins that were found at the project's site. Held 2 feet above the desert surface by two steel posts and cuddled by a paloverde tree in one corner, this structure conveys a sense of longtime residence and belonging in the landscape.

Desert heat is a formidable opponent for any shelter, so Frazee and his team wisely covered the shelter with steel panels attached to metal channels. These channels hold the panels 3 inches away from the wall and provide a shade space where hot air can vent away from the structure, keeping the interior cooler.

For materials, steel and wood (ebony-stained redwood) were selected for their aging qualities and durability in the desert. The rusted steel pays homage to the desert's rich mining history. Over time the panels will acquire a patina similar to that of the desert mountain range surrounding it.

Concrete courtyard and chimney

Frazee explained his reasoning for the door's location: "The entrance to the shelter is intentionally located on the inner courtyard of the concrete pad, close to the chimney mass. This allows an occupant to open up the shelter and gain warmth on a cool night" — either from the nearby fire or from the day's solar heat stored in the slow-release thermal mass. Beyond its heating, cooling, and geographic orientation, I just love the openness of the Miner's Shelter and its surrounding views of the Phoenix Valley on one side and the McDowell Mountain Range on the other. Tiny house, big view.

# THE ALL EIGHTS MICROCABIN

Deek Diedricksen

64 square feet

Stoughton,
Massachusetts

**I** BUILT THE ORIGINAL incarnation of this cabin in 2011 for *The United Stats of America*, a show on the History Channel. I had received a call asking what I could pitch to them, then build, transport to Brooklyn, reassemble, tear down, and drive back to Boston in a mere three or four days. This was no easy feat.

Well, while watching two kids, I was able to moonlight and developed a panelized, prefabricated structure for under $1,000 — and with time to spare. Post-shoot, the network had no use for this little "small-space-trend representation," especially with space at a premium in New York, so it was gifted to me. Score!

What you see now is a far departure from what the cabin originally looked like, and it still continues to change. This little 8 x 8 x 8-foot box not only has a bunk bed for guests but also stands as the tiniest of art galleries for some truly bizarre art, where the paintings and odd flea-market finds are always rotating as I list and sell them on Craigslist. This little side hobby is fun in a treasure-hunting way, and it brings in some additional income, *American Pickers*–style. The All Eights looks different from month to month, and, as a result, I'm never tired of its eclectic decor. Trying not to overfill it with my flea market and roadside hauls — well, that's another story.

ABOVE: **The All Eights lit up at night, a testament to my attraction to clear Tuftex roofing as walls.**

RIGHT: **My brother, Dustin, in an early bare-bones version of the cabin.**

**favorite features**

What I like about this little art locker is that it became a place where I could harbor all the odd, unique, and fun items that normally might not make the cut, stylistically, inside my family home. In the All Eights, the colors don't have to match and there's no one else to judge whether or not a certain piece of art or a vintage Avon-truck-shaped perfume bottle from a yard sale will fit in or not. It's my free-reign, ADD man cave.

The bunk, albeit small, has worked out well. The hut has even been used as a "green room" during film shoots, a place where people could keep warm, grab some grub, or just relax off-set. Also, while not insulated, the All Eights stays rather cozy with just an electric radiator, even in below-freezing weather. I'm no longer such a fan of the curved roof, which I originally loved, and the front "circle hole/square window" experiment is something I wouldn't repeat — it just doesn't look right, nor does it open. But I *do* love the Pet Peek window I later added to the door. Alongside a bright-orange paint job, it gives this place a '70s vibe and spruces up an otherwise boring-looking door (a very old one found on the street).

THE ALL EIGHTS MICROCABIN    81

# THE HINTERLAND STUDIO

Hinterland Design

200 square feet

British Columbia, Canada

**W**HEN A CHILDREN'S BOOK DESIGNER needed a work space separate from the main house, a small and private retreat ended up fitting both the bill and the budget. The challenge in this case was to tear down an existing shed located at the top of a steep hill and replace it with a small studio in the exact same footprint. The homeowner also wanted this new studio to be small yet airy, bright but cozy, and inspirational yet modest. Hinterland Design and founder Riley McFerrin delivered on all counts, especially when it came to an expanse of windows (a whole wall) for natural light. Another success by design was making this space look and feel modern yet in harmony with the rustic charm of the countryside.

With a one-month schedule and a very modest budget, Hinterland Design did a complete demolition of the existing shed and provided the design and build of the new studio from the ground up, including a new foundation, all framing and finishes, new utilities, custom-built workspaces, and even the interior millwork. They were able to incorporate salvaged windows, siding, and doors, as well as repurposed timbers for interior shelving and storage. This helped keep down costs and created that rustic atmosphere. Tucked into the trees, the studio provides expansive views of the ocean through large windows that not only provide light but also inspiration for the artist within.

### favorite features

The Hinterland Studio's sliding outdoor wall, which moves to cover the largest of the windows, is a great idea. I also love the "pop" of the orange door, which gives this little office a dash of character before you even get inside. The natural tongue-and-groove ceiling keeps things light and airy, as the client requested, and the gable-end window brings in a great deal of light. The lack of collar ties in the ceiling space also keeps this place visually uncluttered, while the head, or front edge, of the loft still serves like a collar tie to keep this house plumb and solid. The loft (not shown, at the owner's request) is merely for storage.

# TYLER'S MARSHSIDE SHACK

**Tyler Rodgers**

**32 square feet**

**South Carolina**

**I**'VE RECEIVED a good many e-mails and photos from readers who have gone on to build some of the designs I've offered, or variations of them. Some were just inspired to get out there and try something, which is especially rewarding in cases where the builder has zero previous building experience. Such was the case with 16-year-old Tyler Rodgers, who, when presented with a pile of recycled and scrounged wood, set upon the task of cobbling together a narrow little riverside getaway with a view, all visible from the hammock she strung across the interior of the cabin. Yeah, it was no polished and perfect project, but keep in mind that's not always a bad thing. Some of the more rough and rustic designs I've seen have also been the most infused with character.

Tyler later cleared her original riverside shack to make room for progress: a "step two" tiny house that she designed and built as part of her thesis for her high-school senior project. It's a commendable effort for a 17-year-old (or any new builder!) and shows great growth in a short time span.

LEFT: Tyler's second build (near left) has a much more refined look compared to her first build (far left).

All in all, the budget for this secondary build came in at under $500, due in massive part to a wealth of salvaged materials that Tyler was able to find. This little house has a sleep loft, ample storage, a bathroom, and a couch/daybed, and it still hasn't let go of that amazing view that made the original shack so likable.

**favorite features**

I really admire Tyler's use of raw, unpainted wood in her first project, especially in the wall work where species and stock are mixed (I call this the "calico effect," even if there are more than three looks or colors at play). That said, there's clearly a great deal of progress and growth between her first build, which is more like a fort, and her second one. Structure two is divided into separate living spaces (minuscule as they may be) and has a more cohesive style, some storage space, an actual bed, and even some space set aside for a future bathroom nook. Overall, the two structures are like night and day — but they were built by the same young woman in the span of only a couple of years. She should be proud.

# THE HORROR HUT

**Deek Diedricksen**

**72 square feet**

**Arkham, Massachusetts**

**B**UILT FOR MASSACHUSETTS'S OWN "Minister of Sinister" horror author John Grover during the summer of 2012, the Horror Hut was something I designed as both a writing escape and a greenhouse. How could the two coincide? Well, not only do the generous 6-foot-tall transom windows in front grab a ton of free heat from the daytime sun (the front is south-facing), but those same windows open up to allow the heat to bleed out when John wants things, less, er, "greenhousey."

Gravel floor

This little backyard office employs the following salvaged materials: a roadside door, a single-sash freebie window, four very large windows from Craigslist, and a thick sheet of glass from an old stereo cabinet that I fabricated into yet another side window. I used dark crushed stone for the floor because of its thermal mass (the ability to hold the sun's heat and release it slowly). Furthermore, the floating deck floor is made of cedar, a toss-away from a mill in Vermont, and can be moved in and out of the structure as the owner sees fit.

**favorite features**

The Horror Hut was a case of Craigslist really coming through for me. My brother, Dustin, originally purchased seven(!) 6-foot-tall Andersen windows for a mere $425, and this hut used only four of them. New, these windows would have been close to $1,000 *each*. For the roof I used clear Tuftex polycarbonate roofing, which has really held its own, and it looks great. Polycarbonate, or "polycarb" as it's often called, is used to make bulletproof glass, and I turn to it for its durability, ease of installation, and light weight.

# THE PERISCOPE

**T**HE PERISCOPE STANDS as the first "tree house" I ever built twice! Now hear me out, as, yes, what you see is not in a tree. A while back, I was contacted by a woman who wanted a multi-use tree house cabin built on her property, and seeing as her lot wasn't incredibly close to me, I accepted the gig but under the condition that I could prebuild most of the wall pieces on my own time, in my own backyard. This allowed me to work sporadically when little snippets of time presented themselves (and while listening to heavy metal and drinking beer, if I so desired).

Things progressed nicely, and I planned each piece so that it could be strapped to my little 4 x 8-foot trailer. But somewhere along the line I got carried away with the design, windows, and material use. When the walls were finally good to go and I went to drag them to the trailer, it was clear that my chiropractor was going to be financially thrilled if I continued. I was able to move the four board-and-batten walls, but the idea of singlehandedly hoisting and positioning them high in a tree didn't strike me as very bright . . . or safe.

Deek Diedricksen

39 square feet

Canton,
Massachusetts

**favorite features**

The tall, skinny figure of the Periscope looks cool and unusual during the day, but it's a lanternlike beacon when lit up at night, full of unusual silhouette patterns created by the woodwork and whatever happens to sit on the framed shelves — bottles, a ceramic owl or two, potted plants, and anything else that strikes my collecting fancy. This wall, in effect, becomes a "shadow art" display.

Construction story aside, the Periscope was so named for its tall, skinny façade that comes off as quite a bit taller than it really is. This is partly because its anchored base, only 6 feet x 6 feet 6 inches (just long enough to sneak a bed in) is in such contrast to its height of almost 13 feet. I've also referred to this cabin as the Tetris Tower, since its unusual front window seems to resemble the odd geometric formations from the classic video game.

All said and done, it's just a simple, one-pitch-roof art-studio cabin. Almost three-quarters of the materials were obtained absolutely free through the employment of a little salvaging elbow grease. The plank walls were made from an enormous storm-blown fence that the owner was thrilled to be rid of — two trailer loads of true-inch timbers. The roof was built with the very same wood and covered with the remains of an old aluminum aboveground swimming pool. Furthermore, the windows were found on curbs, while the door was pulled from a 100-year-old cabin in Maine set for demolition. The loft area up top is small but is made more spacious by the recycled window that opens awning-style and gives way to an exterior shelf, upon which you can perch a glass of iced coffee or tea while enjoying a book.

Then and there, so close to being done, I scrapped the entire plan, decided to keep the cabin, and reassembled it in my own yard, ground-bound style. What was one more little structure in my backyard Oompa Loompa village? Thankfully, my wife was supertolerant and didn't kick me out of the house or file for divorce. The tree house I ended up building for this woman is also featured in this book: the Lime Wedge (page 118).

# THE SUNSET HOUSE

**A**FTER QUITTING THEIR JOBS to begin building a cabin in the woods on generations-old family land, Nick Olson and Lilah Horwitz ended up with a getaway that stands as the grand example of being "naturally lighted." Instead of trying to place their windows to chase or frame the sunset, the duo decided to go for an all-windowed approach on the cabin's front wall, beginning with a sash they harvested from an old farm in Pennsylvania. From there, it became a quest of locating, and then framing and fitting, various windows — each with its own origin of interest and its own story to tell. Some windows open, others don't, and the whole assembly comes off as rustically chaotic yet somehow cohesive and well planned at the same time. It's shelter as art — not surprising, as Lilah, a clothing designer, and Nick, a photographer, are both very talented in their respective fields.

**Nick Olson and Lilah Horwitz**

**216 square feet**

**West Virginia**

The Sunset House, a 12 x 18-foot shed-roofed cabin, completed in 2012, became the subject of a short film by the Half Cut Tea production company and soon went semi-viral, with almost one million views in under a year. Again, no surprise, as it's such a strikingly appealing space.

With the cabin's vast wall of glass, the sun might wake you sooner than you had planned in the Sunset House, but who could complain when greeted with that expansive vista? I suppose you might think, "But what about privacy?" But if you're deep in the middle of nowhere, the beauty is that you probably wouldn't need, or want, curtains. The raccoons might see what you've been up to, but who are they gonna tell?

Being a fan of natural wood, I'm also very glad that this place wasn't hastily slapped with an interior paint job. Paint has its time and place, but with great paint also comes great responsibility — the upkeep, the touch-ups, the time and money to coat a place to begin with, and so on. The cliché "less is more" certainly holds true in this case.

# THE COLLAPSIBLE HOUSE

**W**EIGHING IN at a mere 170 pounds, with the added attraction of being completely foldable for storage and transport, comes this neat little answer to temporary housing, potentially for camping or even the homeless. Setup takes all of about 15 minutes, with two or even one person. This unassuming little shelter breaches the barrier between shed and tent (a shent?). Add in a folding table, a swivel lamp stand that folds against the wall, a screened window or two, and even a mount on which to display your iPad's fireplace app, and you have the makings of a cozy little getaway or refuge from the wind and rain. Kathy claims that even in winds over 25 miles per hour, this luggable little shelter holds up just fine.

Kathy Dekker

56 square feet

Wisconsin

## favorite features

The fact that it's merely four sheets of solid plywood — connected with a spline and braced with various "plug-in" hardware and boards — makes the Collapsible House beyond easy and affordable. It is little more than a spacious, rigid tent, but it's certainly fun and clever. A souped-up version of this might be a viable option for disaster-relief shelters.

# THE BREAD BOX

**B** **UILT AT A HANDS-ON WORKSHOP** I hosted in late 2013, the Bread Box was named for its resemblance to the bread cubbies of old that would hang beneath a cupboard. Take that shape, flip it over, and you more or less have the basis for this tiny little structure. It's meant as a backwoods or backyard office, a greenhouse, or a minicamp for weekend retreats. No, it doesn't have a bathroom, kitchen, servants' quarters, wine cellar, or billiards room, but even as a mere 6 x 8-foot shelter it feels rather large inside because of its abundance of windows and, therefore, natural light.

Deek Diedricksen

48 square feet

Canton, Massachusetts

As with many of my designs, the aim was ease of construction, flexibility of use, and affordability. This entire cabin could be built for somewhere in the ballpark of $700. It has a very basic platform base, a framed wall skinned with poplar plywood sides, and really nothing more. I chose to frame the door-end wall with 2x6s, instead of the standard 2x4s, for their added depth. The walls were also framed horizontally so they offer several layers of shelving, and all are supported with debarked maple limbs for a rustic tie-in. Apart from this one Adirondack-style nod, the Bread Box is really a very modern outbuilding.

The art on the back wall is one of many large pieces I've made out of what would otherwise be trash — little scraps of trimmed, painted wood saved from my projects over the years. Yes, while I save just about everything, I *use* just about everything. The smallest of unpainted scraps, those I actually deem worthless, wind up heating my home via my central woodstove. I call this the Hotdog Approach: *everything* gets used.

Floors made from beadboard

**favorite features**

You wouldn't know it, but almost the entire base of the Bread Box is built from free, found dimensional lumber and pallet wood — pressure-treated, too! You just can't beat that price. The floors are clad, rather unusually, with antique bead-board. This style of tongue-and-groove board is usually reserved for walls, but I felt it would make a great floor. I overcame the challenges of its crumb-catching grooves by slapping on some polyurethane with a hardener additive. By applying a few coats, I eventually filled and leveled out the channels and wound up with a nice, glossy, flat floor. Again, by thinking outside the box and breaking a conventional rule or two, I found a means to an attractive, budget-friendly end.

# SLEEPBOX

Arch Group

100 square feet

Various locations

**F**ROM A TEAM of Russian architects known as the Arch Group comes this wildly modern and compact sleeping unit aptly named Sleepbox. Marketed to transportation facilities such as railway stations and airports, this sleek, lunchbox-shaped snooze chamber comes complete with a fold-out desk, bunk beds, ample power to charge your laptop and cell phone, and, yes, heavy shades for privacy. Better yet, these affordable temporary relief stations are soundproofed, air conditioned, come in an expansive variety of colors, and take up so little space that they hardly interfere with retail areas or pedestrian traffic.

These modern microhuts can be located either indoors or out and are aimed at saving time, money, and energy for weary travelers dealing with layovers. At airports they can save you from having to book a costly hotel room, take a cab back and forth, recheck your bags, and pass through security again — all for far less money than conventional lodging.

Oh yeah, they're also fully loaded with Wi-Fi, TVs, and gaming systems and come in single, twin, and double units.

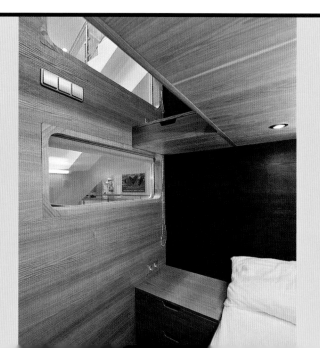

**favorite features**

Layover or not, I'd like to go to an airport just to check into one of these things. And I have to say, the Sleepbox is just begging to be turned into a jaw-dropping tree house. I'm also a fan of the little storage nooks and pull-down workspaces. These take up little or no visual space and almost zero room when folded away. "Out of sight, out of mind" is an important adage to remember when designing something so very tiny.

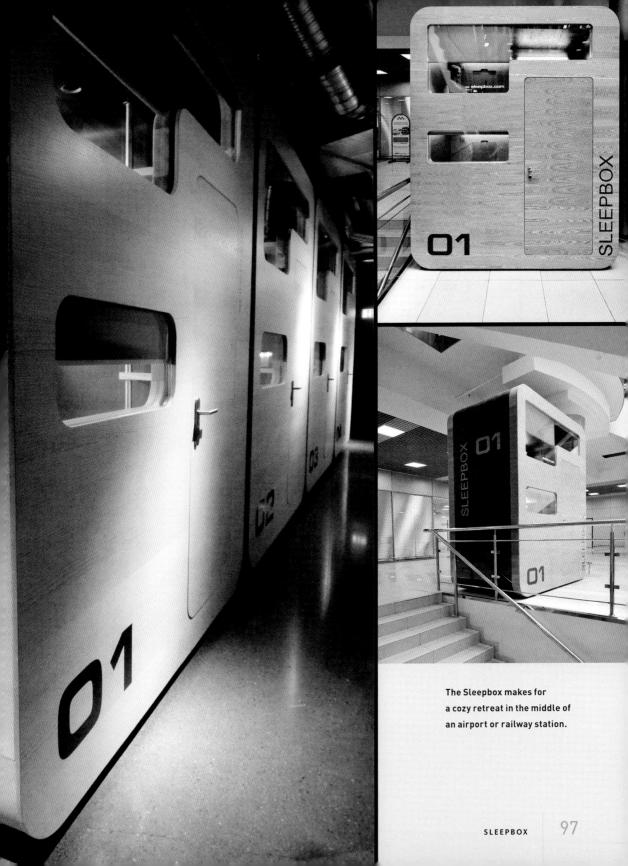

The Sleepbox makes for
a cozy retreat in the middle of
an airport or railway station.

# NEIL AND KURT'S TEENAGE LOG CABIN

**Neil and Kurt Malek**

**120 square feet**

**Jewett City, Connecticut**

**T**HIS RUSTIC LOG CABIN was built by Neil and Kurt Malek (my cousins) as teenagers in the mid-'90s, with help from one of their good friends, Mark Polanski. The simple structure has been sitting alone, deep in the woods of Connecticut, for almost two decades now and has held up remarkably well considering the harsh winters. I revisited the site in 2013 and snapped a few photos. Inside, there's a Scandia woodstove, which was donated to my cousins' project by my father, Glenn. This stove was the very unit that used to heat our home when I was a boy.

According to Neil, the footprint of the cabin was around 10 x 12 feet, with a standing height of about 7 feet (they dug the floor down about 6 inches so they wouldn't have to build up as much) and the peak of the roof somewhere around 12 feet. They built the whole thing by hand, without any power tools. "We cut the trees with a bow saw and notched all the logs with an axe so they fit snugly," says Neil. "We then chinked between the logs using a mix of mud from the swamp nearby (a few hundred feet downhill) and grass clippings from our yard. The roofing was my aunt's old pine flooring that she gave us when she redid her floors (with tar paper laid underneath)."

Kurt hollowed out a large log to use as a sink and made a drain hole in the bottom, complete with a hose that emptied outside the cabin into a hole covered by a stone. They used slab wood (left over from cutting logs into boards) from a sawmill down the road to fill in the gable triangle above the door and in back. Another friend gave them deer furs that they salted and dried and hung in the loft as cushioning "until the critters got into them."

Neil remembers staying overnight in the cabin, even in the winter. "If you got the stove ripping, that place would get darn hot even with the holes in the walls. We used to cook on that stovetop, too, and cleaned the pots and pans in that sink, which, like the woodstove, is still sitting up there in the woods to this day."

**favorite features**

This is a pretty impressive project for three kids, all under 18 years of age at the time. Kurt, the youngest, was around 14. As small as it was, the cabin had a simple horseshoe-shaped loft that slept three. Digging the floor down to limit the number of logs to be cut for the wall (a laborious and time-consuming task) is also a common and clever tactic. This log cabin doesn't have a stone starter base as most would, but it still holds up rather well without one, nearly 20 years later.

# AUSTIN GUEST HOUSE

Jennifer Francis

96 square feet

Austin, Texas

**I**N 2013 I WAS SENT DOWN to Austin, Texas, to teach a class on small-scale design and building with free, salvaged, and recycled items. Well, as "Keep Austin Weird" has been this city's ongoing slogan and mindset for some time now, it was no shock that I soon found an abundance of cool, funky, backyard cabins and studios to visit — and visit I did! Jennifer Francis's little rental unit stood out to me, and although my visit was brief, I really dug the vibe of this place, which is simple, colorful, and built on an extremely small budget.

This little backyard retreat is occasionally rented out on airbnb.com and features a few wallet-friendly renovations (from its initial shed state) that are worthy of mention. The porch sports a pair of columns rescued from a neighbor's 1930s Sears-Roebuck catalog house, and "every stick of furniture was nabbed from garage sales," says Jennifer. She and her father wired the structure for electricity, built in a lofted sleep space (you can also sleep down below on the couch), and gave it all a very rustic and natural look with an abundance of old fence planks. Yes, what you see as interior siding is made of slats from a pile of fence wood!

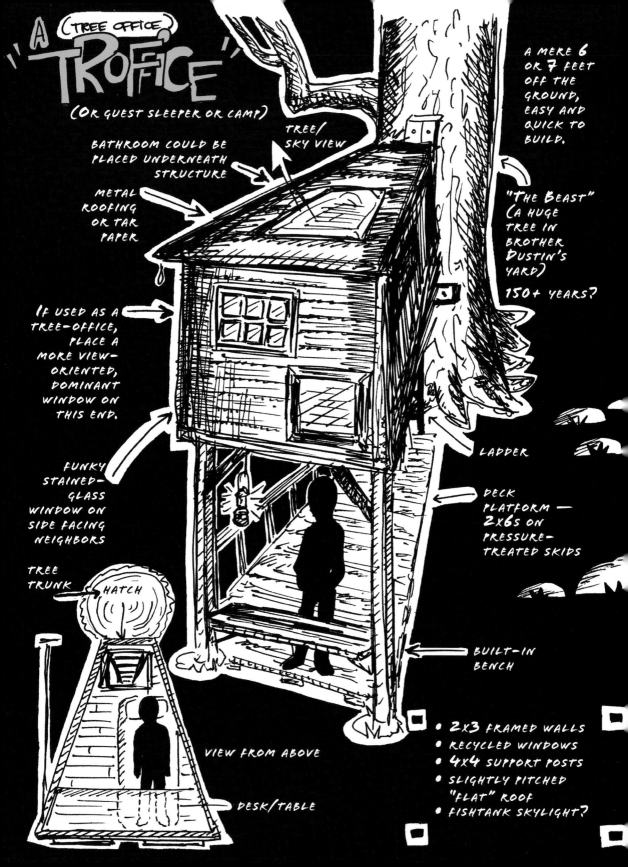

# tree houses & stilted shelters

## 3

**I HAPPEN TO BE QUITE A FAN OF TREE HOUSES,** and the majority of my client calls and design gigs tend to fall within this subgenre of shelter. It should come as no surprise, then, that there are a few tree houses between these covers, and while I can't pick one as a favorite, the ones you see here are among the best. My personal criteria for inclusion are that they be financially accessible and not too traditional in shape, scope, or style (it just gets boring), and that they also have a homey, cozy, and self-built look about them. Million-dollar tree houses (there are plenty of books on them) are unrealistic for most people and often lack the childlike whimsy and charm of their more affordable counterparts.

# SCHAUMBURG TREE HOUSE

Daniel Alexander
and Mike
Marshall

110 square feet

Schaumburg,
Illinois

**B** **UILT AND DESIGNED** by Daniel Alexander and his buddy Mike Marshall, the Schaumburg Tree House, just outside of Chicago, is also a nightly lodge. This aerial inn boasts air-conditioning and a twin sleeping loft, as well as a microwave, coffee-maker, fridge, high-end Pella windows, a private deck, outdoor shower, kitchenette, and sink — all suspended, without a single stilt or pole, 15 feet up in the crook of a backyard tree. As if that doesn't make it attractive enough, the house overlooks a waterfall, a koi pond, and a lawn-bowling court. Talk about roughin' it! It's far from the scavenged-wood plank hut you might have had as a kid, yet for all its fanciness it retains a ton of homemade, rustic, down-to-earth charm.

**favorite
features**

The minuteness of the Schaumburg
Tree House's railed sleep loft,
reached by a simple, sturdy wooden
ladder, just begs the guest to climb
up with a good book and hole up for
a while. It's very nestlike — small
but inviting. Some may think it's
just too tiny, but for sleeping only,
how much space do you really
need? The fire pole to the ground
also adds a little dash of childlike
whimsy to an otherwise very adult
tree house escape.

Fire pole

# SWANKY SAN FRANCISCO TREE HOUSE

**Doug Studebaker**

**80 square feet**

**Burlingame, California**

**F**ROM THE FIRST TIME I approached Doug Studebaker's tree house overlooking San Francisco Bay, it was nuthin' but love. The locale, the interior decor, the overall vibe . . . Doug got everything right.

This tree house, where you can stay in bed-and-breakfast style, is but 80 square feet. Sounds tight for a family, right? Well, add in a partial wraparound deck, a sleep loft (not standing height, and not counted in the overall square footage), a daybed below for those who don't want to make the climb, and an ample arrangement of windows, and you have a good example of small-space trickery at its finest. Lots of light, a high ceiling, and plenty of visual openness all contribute to a spacious mood. And there's no forgetting that you're in a tree, either, as part of the tree's trunk and several enormous limbs pass right through the very room you stay in.

I really appreciate the fact that Doug left the entire tree unharmed in his design. Granted, with the West Coast's much larger trees, tree housing is an easier game there than in the East, but it nevertheless takes a good deal of planning, and to do it without altering the tree deserves mention. Doug's clever flashing (polyethylene hose tubing) around a limb that passes through the middle of a Plexiglas window, as well as his mini heater — a thin, ceramic, wall-mounted affair — are among many less conventional things I admire about this place. This tree house even has a TV and DVD player (which I didn't dare use, as it just seemed like cheating the tree house experience). The bathroom is in a private nook of the main house about 25 feet away. There, guests also have access to a quaint little kitchenette all their own, where a window perfectly frames a view of the tree house.

# FERN FOREST TREE HOUSE

Harrison
Reynolds
(and son)

120 square feet

Lincoln, Vermont

**D** EEP IN THE WOODS outside Bristol, Vermont, lies a quaint little tree house that was designed and built by retired woodworking teacher Harrison Reynolds and his son. This lofted lodge (another one you can stay in via airbnb.com) is a dream-made-reality of Reynolds's, alongside author and host extraordinaire Ellie Bryant. In a short span of time the two have made this micro-inn rather famous. It is fame well deserved, too.

Tree growing
through
center of
house

Spend a night at the Fern Forest Tree House and you'll be treated to a gorgeous view, use of a hot tub, an incredible locally sourced breakfast in a beautiful sunroom, and woods galore to stroll in. But the biggest treat is the house's interior. It immediately convinces you to sit down, relax, and enjoy simply being there. The private, queen-size loft, while a little difficult to ascend to, is cozy and boasts an even better view. If you still prefer not to make the climb, Harrison and Ellie have you covered with a daybed down below.

## favorite features

At the end of its great approach — a long ramp leading 30 feet up into a grove of maples overlooking a deer path in the valley below — the Fern Forest Tree House greets you with its front door, a beautiful stained-glass art piece crafted by Harrison himself, a tribute piece in the style of Frank Lloyd Wright. In my travels, my family and I have stayed in a variety of unusual places — from houseboats to funky, hippie-style backyard cottages — but my kids have particularly fond memories of Fern Forest. "Dad," my son said, "I love how they have a tree growing right through the center of the room!" It is a nice touch, and a reminder at all times that you are sleeping 30 feet over the forest floor.

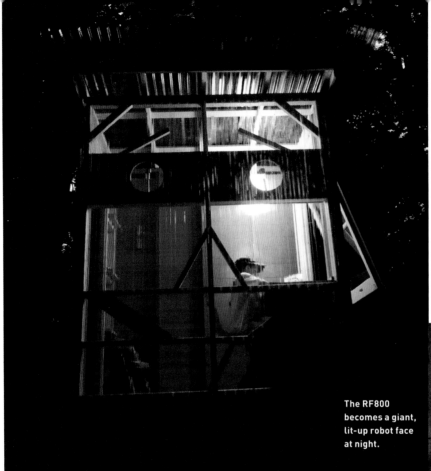

Solar lamps become the eyes of the robot.

The RF800 becomes a giant, lit-up robot face at night.

# THE RF 800

"**JUST BUILD PRETTY MUCH** whatever you want, as long as you make it funky." Those are words I love to hear from a client, and more or less what I was told regarding this build near downtown Boston. My guidelines were that it had to be up in a tree (two oaks in this case), have a clear roof, and be big enough for two or three kids and their sleeping bags. I convinced the owner to let me make it versatile enough so that one day the adults could use this structure as a lofted office, and that was that: the RF 800 (short for Robot Face $800) was born. By the time I completed this project, in the summer of 2014, I had begun wishing it were *my* office. It was great to see the kids fall in love with this place, and their mother, initially unsure about a giant robot head in her backyard, also came around when the tree house was finished and all lit up at night.

Deek Diedricksen

28 square feet

Boston area, Massachusetts

The Robot Face tree house sits uphill from the owners' main home and is perfectly framed in their kitchen sink window. This way, while mom or dad cooks or washes dishes, they're able to see what the kids are up to. The tree house's clear front wall even allows a view within (and could be curtained for sleepovers). The see-through roof offers a view of the oak boughs above, and the removable desk, placed right in front of a swinging window, has its own great view. This whimsical shelter has solar light-up eyes, and it's functional too. The open framing creates an abundance of shelving for knickknacks, toys, or, later, office supplies.

Instead of trimming an extra-long board, I left it as it was and attached a swing.

# THE STEAM STUDIO

Helle Kvamme

34 square feet

Finland

**T**HIS IS ONE OF THE FEW HUTS in this book that is more art than functional space. I mean, how long do you expect your desktop paperwork to last in a sauna? Regardless, I found the imagery striking, and as for a steam-filled tree house workspace, your first question might be "Why?" You might also ask, "Why not?"

Finnish artist Helle Kvamme created the Steam Studio in 2007 as a part of an international art exchange by SKART-Ireland. The project was called PLUS/MINUS, based on the idea that the steam would raise the temperature in the studio from negative to positive degrees. "While working in the studio, I had to fire up a woodstove to steam water," Kvamme explained to me. "The steam went up through a pipe in the floor and changed the dry, cold air to moist, warm air. Soon enough, the

steam made fog on the glass and then the place became more private. I simply became a shadow in the space at night. When I stopped firing the stove, the place got cold again, and the window became icy on the inside, distorting the image of the room."

Kvamme used recycled materials where possible, including the large windows, which were given to her by a neighbor. The result was a space surrounded by nature, where she could concentrate on the details of all the things around her.

**favorite features**

The Steam Studio is certainly whimsical and creative, but take the steam away, and it would make for a very affordable tree house office in the woods — albeit with no privacy, but therein may lie the beauty. Sliding doors are surprisingly abundant on Craigslist and roadsides, so making something like this is a very doable project. Plus, with a spectacular view in the middle of the woods, it would be really fun to spend time inside. Or how about in the middle of a breathtaking marsh? A word of warning, though: unless you like yourself well-done, you'd be wise to build something like this in the shade.

# TREE HOUSE ON A FARM

Janice Sorensen

120 square feet

Buckland,
Massachusetts

**J**ANICE SORENSEN'S tree house is another simple, well-executed affair that feels far more spacious inside than it appears (being only 10 x 12 feet). Part of this illusion is due to the generous use of windows, which I feel a tree house should always have plenty of. After all, what's the point of being up in a tree if you're not reminded that you're aloft? It's like building a beach house without working in a view of the water.

Originally built as a triangular tent platform, over time this structure morphed into a full-out tree house on a reconfigured square base. Now available as a rental through airbnb. com, Janice's tree house has hosted numerous guests from around the US, all of them looking for the unique experience of spending the night in a tree — and on a majestic farm with a mountain view to boot! This Buckland tree escape is both clever and thrifty in its decor and design. The floor, mere plywood, has been adorned with the stenciled shapes of leaves, many from the host tree itself. Janice and her husband and hired carpenter, Marcus Fisher, have made good use of budget-friendly slab wood, the less desirable cuts from a mill. These boards not only serve as exterior cladding for this two-season tree lodge, they've also been made into handsome and rustic window trim within.

I really dig the natural limbs that make up one corner of the bed, the entrance hatch that allows for easy access (despite its use of floor space), and the surprisingly high ceilings that help create a feeling of spaciousness. With the clear Tuftex polycarbonate roofing it's almost like living outdoors while actually being within.

mileage out of this thing?" And that's exactly what I had in mind with this little wedge-shaped cabin.

The Lime Wedge is a mere 6 feet 6 inches wide and only 6 feet deep, but it seems to feel quite a bit bigger because the height is a full 8 feet. This enabled me to use full lengths of standard-size lumber, which means fewer cuts and less waste, saving me money, time, and hassle. After you pass through a tiny 5-foot 6-inch door that downsizes expectations, the 8-foot interior feels rather enormous, and the clear roof lets in massive amounts of natural light, adding to the trickery. No, the tree house doesn't overheat in the summer, as it's built under the canopy of a pair of very large maple trees. When wintertime rolls around and the leaves drop, you're able to take advantage of free solar heat through the roof.

The front "headlight" windows are light hoods from a car dealership lot. I pulled them out of a scrapyard dumpster. All the other windows, except for the low, basement-style front window, were found on the side of the road. Best of all, the beadboard exterior walls (treated with a UV-blocking stain) came from my neighbors' house as they tore out their 100-year-old living room — a nice piece of history added to the build.

# THE LIME WEDGE

**Deek Diedricksen**

**42 square feet**

**Newton, Massachusetts**

**T**HE LIME WEDGE (aka "The Newton") is a tree house, or "pole cabin" to tree house purists, that I built for a client in the fall of 2013. Like many of my builds, it was designed for multiple uses. I often find myself asking the client, "But what about when your kid grows up? Don't you still want to get some versatile

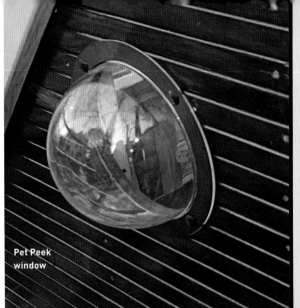

Pet Peek window

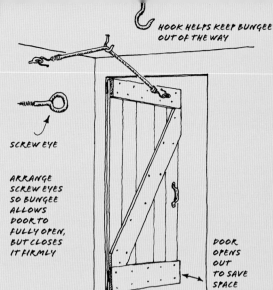

HOOK HELPS KEEP BUNGEE OUT OF THE WAY

SCREW EYE

ARRANGE SCREW EYES SO BUNGEE ALLOWS DOOR TO FULLY OPEN, BUT CLOSES IT FIRMLY

DOOR OPENS OUT TO SAVE SPACE

**favorite features**

Yes, the wood for the Lime Wedge's walls came with a price — seven hours of pulling nails and cleaning it up — but I've worked this enormous score into quite a few projects, including the Crate Escape (page 158), the Bread Box (page 94), and the Professor's Pod (page 140). The labor eventually paid for itself ten times over. Not only that, but I honestly find this kind of work enjoyable. I can sit there with an iced tea, listen to the radio, and begin a soothing round of mindless work, all outside in the sun and fresh air. Plus, I get a certain satisfaction from knowing that I'm giving new life to walls and wood that otherwise would be rotting in the town dump.

Another thing that worked rather well is the little bungee-cord rig I set up for the door. Knowing that most kids are apt to fail to close the door, and that winds will blow open a latch-less hatch sooner or later, I simply took a 99-cent bungee cord and attached its hook ends to two eye screws, then added a hook in the middle to hold the cord out of the way of the door. It worked like a charm. Every time someone enters the tree house, the door closes right behind them. You can easily adjust the speed at which the door closes by setting the eye screws at different distances. All said, it takes about three minutes to install.

# THE MODFRUGAL STILT HOUSE

ModFruGal

**64 square feet**

Nashville,
Tennessee

**S**OME PURISTS of the architectural subgenre of tree houses believe that a true tree house must be at least 20 feet in the air and can be supported only by trees — no posts allowed. Well, this one satisfies neither criterion and might rightly be called a "stilt cabin," but really, who the heck cares? What matters is that it's just a good-looking project.

Perched a good 10 or 12 feet in the air near the city limits of Nashville, yet far from the noise and congestion of downtown, this cabin certainly has a modern feel to it. That's no surprise,

as the house's builder-owner heads up the cleverly titled blog ModFruGal. The 8 x 8-foot structure was designed as a building project and destination for both kids *and* adults and, while sparse and simple, also harbors some great design tips and ideas: framing that doubles as shelving, homemade sliding Plexiglas windows, a swinging fan mount for humid weather, and a space-saving stacked mattress setup (one stores under the other when not in use). And though it's rather modern in look, this Tennessee tree house still manages to blend in well with the woods around it.

Railing screens
made of hog panel

**favorite features**

The hog-panel railing screens on ModFruGal's mini-deck are a great economical idea. Who would think that caging designed for livestock (thick screen mesh sold at agricultural stores) could look so good and so modern, work so well, and yet cost so little? The overall color scheme of this place, including the blood-orange deck chairs contrasted against the dark brown exterior, is also funky yet cohesive.

121

# THE WOLFE'S DEN

**Deek Diedricksen**

**75 square feet**

**New Paltz, New York**

**N**AMED AFTER THE NEW YORK CITY ATTORNEY who hired me for this build (and who had a gorgeous stone cottage on a piece of land upstate), the Wolfe's Den was designed, prefabricated, transported, and assembled all before I had a chance to meet Ms. Wolfe. Luckily, when she arrived at the end of the assembly, she absolutely loved the structure and has been using this reading-room-in-a-tree ever since. It is also intended as a sleep space for her nephews on occasional visits and is wired for electricity and heat.

The unusually shaped Wolfe's Den — a triangle just for the fun of it! — is only about 5 feet off the ground and is accessed via a few steps to a little deck just big enough for a pair of chairs and a grill. The deck extends the limited indoor living space to the outdoors. Once inside, the occupant is greeted with a sparse but colorful setup: a small armchair, a mini built-in daybed, some permanent shelving and decor elements, and a variety of pieces and pillows that add color and a vibrant feel to this small space. With the clear ceiling showing trees around and above you, the feeling of being in a tree is undeniable.

**favorite features**

The Wolfe Den is small but feels larger because of its almost 360-degree view. I should also add that all the windows and the French door were freebies found on the side of the road. A fun addition is the "voyeuristic bird feeder," an IKEA glass fruit bowl mounted upside-down over a routed hole in the floor. From your seat in the armchair, you can view the birds feeding on a seed tray that hangs below the dome, but they can't see you. Best of all, this little perk costs almost nothing to make.

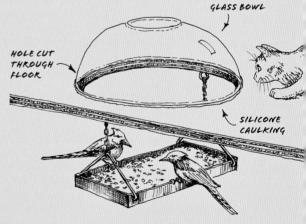

GLASS BOWL

HOLE CUT THROUGH FLOOR

SILICONE CAULKING

# NASHVILLE MODERN FORT

Bjon Pankratz

200 square feet

Nashville,
Tennessee

**B** JON PANKRATZ'S IDEA of a break from nearly seven years of reno-vation on his family home was to take on what was to become a fairly massive kids' fort project. So much for downtime and relaxation! Having dubbed it a tree house (though it isn't one in true form), Pankratz let his imagination fly with this one, and there's no denying he's a fan of both trim and wild angles. Even at a glance, it's clear this two-story backyard playscape is no ordinary weekend impulse project born in the aisles of the local hardware store. Standing almost 15 feet high, this modern microstructure is quite impressive. A tree passes gracefully through its entirety, too, in effect making it a very different sort of tree house.

A tree centerpiece

**favorite features**

What's not to love? The Nashville Modern Fort has artistic angles galore and a look of being both carefully planned and off-the-cuff, a balance some strive very hard to achieve. The fort is clearly modern in style, but the tree passing through it seems to ground it and add a dash of the rustic, keeping it from looking overly fancy.

# JONAS'S TREE HOUSE

Jonas Diedricksen

18 square feet

Canton,
Massachusetts

**I** **HAVE A SOFT SPOT** in my heart for junk-fabricated, funky, colorful, hokey, ad-lib structures (just in case you hadn't noticed yet!). There are so many great ones out there, and they can be found by paying just the slightest attention while on any road trip. This particular example is located rather close to my home — about 40 feet away. My son Jonas built it at age six, and it was his introduction to many tools and techniques, as well as to the notion of me letting him succeed — and make mistakes — on his own. One valuable lesson learned (after a trip to the doctor) was not to leave boards on the ground with nails sticking out of them. He had been warned, but I think he'll now be ten times as careful!

I couldn't have been prouder when Jonas asked, "Dad, can you grab me those kitchen cabinet doors?" I was stopped on the side of the road to retrieve some "architectural salvage" (free junk windows) for an upcoming build, and Jonas was clearly doing his own scouting. "I think they'd make a great door for my tree house." Add in some Tuftex roofing scraps I gave him, an assortment of 2x4s that he gleaned from a "take me" pile behind a hardware store, and a deck (the one small thing I helped him with) made of nothing but scrap wood that otherwise would have been kindling, and this little structure provided months of entertainment. What's really great is that in an age of Mountain Dew–guzzling, video-game-hypnotized kids, Jonas wanted nothing but to be able to work on his tree house day after day. Perhaps he, and his carpenter sidekick sister, Angie, will be able to look back at this someday and have a good giggle, and be reminded, "Oh yeah, Dad *did* let us do some cool things when we were little!"

**favorite features**

It's my kid's tree house, so of course I love it (not so sure the neighbors do!), but I particularly like that kitchen-cabinet door, the artwork and names of clubhouse "members" that have been scrawled on it, and the floor — a recycled forklift pallet. He also got quite creative with the random items he attached to its exterior to "make it more fun and colorful": paint can lids, a free Frisbee from a fair, an old set of wind chime beads, and anything else he could scrounge up. The calico look of the boards on his exterior wall was a reminder to me of how good a multitude of scrap-wood pieces could look. This later served as re-inspiration for my "wild wall" approach in the Relax Shack (page 73).

# By Land or Sea...

This should actually read "By Land, Sea, or in a Tree," as a structure this lightweight and easy to build could work for any of those scenarios. The key to this one is to use thin, light frame lumber and thin plywood — but with bracing, glue, and waterproofing.

FOR ROAD USE...
A BIKE/TRAILER HITCH

CORRUGATED CLEAR PLASTIC
ROOFING/HATCH

REPURPOSED    2x3
SASH          BASE FR[...]

FOLD-DOWN
LEVELING LEGS

HEAVY-DUTY MOUNTAIN BIKE TIRES

ROAD REFLECTORS

ROOF OPENS FOR SHADE
WHEN NOT MOVING

THE SHANTYBOAT
VERSION
(BIKE CART SANS
WHEELS)

EXTEND ROO[...]
FOR SUN
PROTECTION

ADDED
HOMEMADE
PONTOONS AND
DECK SPACE

# on
# wheels

## 4

**THESE DAYS, BUILDING "ON WHEELS"** seems to be the trend, and in many regions it's a subtle way to circumvent building codes. If a tiny house isn't allowed in a particular town (due to minimum square footage laws, for example), but camping or parked RVs *are* allowed, tiny houses on wheels may stand in a gray area between the two. Should the authorities or complaining neighbors come knocking, or should you be suddenly overcome with the desire to plop yourself in a new locale, your home already doubles as a moving van. Just batten down the hatches, secure the breakables, and you're ready to go! However, in order to be roadworthy, a tiny house must be built to handle high wind loads. Also, it can't be over 8 feet 6 inches wide and 13 feet 6 inches tall; otherwise, you need special permits from the Department of Transportation to take it on the highway. Still, there's a lot that can be done within the confines of such a small space, even with shacks that are not meant to be full-time dwellings, or those that will never hit the open road.

# SHEPHERD'S HUTS

Plankbridge
Hutmakers

28 square feet
(and up)

Dorchester in
Dorset, UK

**P**LANKBRIDGE HUTMAKERS BEGAN in Richard Lee's furniture-making workshop. He was searching for an "outdoor room" design that could be replicated yet have a custom-made feel about it. Inspiration came from an old shepherd's hut that stood for many years on a hill close to where the writer Thomas Hardy lived, and soon Richard Lee and Jane Dennison had built a replica on a set of old wheels. The traditional shepherd's hut, originally used by a solitary shepherd while tending his sheep, seemed to have potential for a wide range of modern-day uses. The duo's fairly rustic reproductions later evolved into Plankbridge's highly insulated timber-frame huts. Despite the modern twist, Plankbridge is still keen to keep true to the heritage of the originals, as you can see.

**favorite features**

The vaulted roof of the Plankbridge shepherd's huts, like that of many gypsy wagons and vardos of old, lends itself well to small structures, softening the effects of edges: you gain height and also eliminate the in-your-face lines that tell you, "Here is where the peak is, and this is where the walls top out." It's a subtle way to create a feeling of spaciousness. In addition, I really like the old-world-meets-new approach in their design, not to mention the timber framing, clean lines, and woodworking. It is simplicity in fine form.

# THE CUB

**Deek Diedricksen**

**40 square feet**

**Boston, Massachusetts**

**T**HE CUB, A SHED-ROOFED microhut on wheels, is something I toyed around with between projects for other clients. Could I design something affordable, simple to build, multifunctional, *and* able to be fastened atop a single-axle trailer? To complicate matters, could this structure be towed by my Chrysler minivan (the ultimate in super-cool vehicles, I know)? In the end the mission was accomplished, and this 40-square-foot trailer has weathered a few long road trips already, including

a nine-hour round-trip trek to Vermont's Yestermorrow Fair and back, dirt-road mountain pass and all. I originally built the Cub on wheels to take advantage of a permit loophole (it's an "RV" or "trailer load" and not an accessory building) and never really intended it to be a gas-guzzling, not-so-aerodynamic commute cabin. Nonetheless, it has handled things rather well.

As for the build, since wind loads can be a concern when traveling, all the plywood is screwed *and* glued to the 2x4 framing, which is further strengthened with knee braces and assorted hardware. Since I love the trash-to-treasure spirit, I used a roadside find for the large side window and got the 100-year-old beadboard wall from a neighbor's house that was under renovation. The entire ceiling is clad in old fence wood (the work of hurricane Sandy in a nearby town). Come to think of it, I should send a bottle of wine to the guy who let me take two trailerloads of this lumber off his hands for absolutely nothing! As for the bunk bed, it was designed at 6 feet 4 inches to fit my frame. It's a little on the thin side, truth be told, so as not to sacrifice what little standing room a mere 5 x 8-foot trailer can offer. Remember, every inch counts when designing and outfitting such small spaces.

**favorite features**

I'm very content with many aspects of the Cub, as, naturally, I chose them for my own tastes and reasons. Things I'd change? Well, I might build it a little shorter so I wouldn't worry about it tipping over (although it's never felt like it would, even at sharp turns). This would decrease both weight and lumber cost. Also, people rarely believe that I can fit in the bunk, but I've spent a few nights in it, and it works. Making this bunk lower and a hair wider might be a good move, but all in all, I'm pretty happy with it. The storage (or lower bed platform), which doubles as stairs to the bunk, also works out nicely. Basically it's a poor man's version of Japanese *tansu* steps (hollow stairs with storage within or under). This step (or steps, if you add a second box) is merely a wooden IKEA storage crate, which are affordable, good-looking, and very strong. But any wooden box, as long as it's built soundly, would suffice.

# THE GNOMADIK

Adam Szoke and
Chris Boux

70 square feet

Vancouver Island,
British Columbia,
Canada

**H**ERE'S ANOTHER CASE where art and shelter exist as one. Builder/designers Adam Szoke and Chris Boux started to envision this beautiful dwelling on wheels after picking up a travel-trailer frame at a scrap-metal yard. Using Google's SketchUp drafting program to send drawings back and forth, they designed a comfortable, spacious, and versatile space within the confines of a 7 x 10-foot platform and very limited capital.

While winter storms raged outside, Adam and Chris worked in the shop, milling old cedar fence panels and weathered fir boards for siding and windows. They even went so far as to build and frame their own custom windows, which was time-consuming but proved to be a big money-saver in the end. The abundance of light-colored wood inside comes from specially selected construction-grade 2x4s and 2x6s that Adam and Chris planed down to the required dimensions. "Remilling was a lot of work," says Adam, "but when you have a lot of time and very little money, it's well worth it, especially for the final look."

Unique front door

Shelving that works as steps

From conception to completion, building the micro-cottage took almost nine months, the bulk of the time taken up by the interior. "Because the space is so small we had to consider every square inch of detail," explains Adam. "We had a lot of fun creating unique solutions, like the four-fold table, the modular bench seat, or the pull-out step boxes and floating step shelves." The tiles over the sink were made from an old piece of aluminum from a water tank, brushed and burnished. Chris's masterful inlay work even includes "a small hidden gem box held in by rare earth magnets, which can only be spotted if you know exactly where to look."

**favorite features**

Well, upon first glance, the Gnomadik's main attraction, fittingly, is Adam's handcrafted, one-of-a-kind door. Beyond that, I love the dual-purpose shelves/steps in this little cottage on wheels, and the fact that in a mere 7 x 10 feet Adam and crew have managed to fit a five-seater kitchen table, a sleep loft, and a rather beautiful gravity-fed water system for the kitchen sink. The secret compartment — I'm a sucker for these things — adds a bit of childlike fun to the whole design.

# THE MIGHTY MICRO HOUSE

**Angela Ramseyer**

**136 square feet**

**Freeland, Washington**

"**B Y THE TIME** the tiny house concept found me," Angela Ramseyer says, "I had already become something of a cyclical downsizer." She had left her Seattle desk job to take up residence in a 100-square-foot Whidbey Island tool shed, so she wasn't fazed when the cabinetmaker next door asked if she'd be interested in building a tiny house on wheels. Instead, she was hooked.

Angela had no prior carpentry experience, but she "scraped, scavenged, and toiled" and gradually learned to handle the tools. Initially she had trouble finding a suitable used trailer, so instead she acquired a temporary set of axles "in order to ward off permitting questions." She was eventually led to her trailer a year later by two escaped horses who ran up her driveway: "I went to tell the next-door neighbors about their horses and there spied the rusty, peeling, flat-tired, rotten-planked trailer of my dreams moldering under a refuse pile." She bought it, got rid of the rotten decking, regreased its bearings, replaced the tires, scraped and repainted the frame, and rewired its brake lights. One year later, the little house was lowered onto its new foundation.

Scavenging for materials became one of Angela's favorite parts of the project: "At first, learning to see these things was like hunting for mushrooms. You go to the places where they would ideally lurk and look for hours in vain. Finally, as you're just about to give up, you spot one! The second find becomes easier. Then you eventually develop an eye for it and begin to see salvage finds everywhere." These items add character to her home. Her favorites include the loft's half-round leaded window and an old woodstove door covering the cook fan.

Curtained cabinets — even burlap sacks will do!

**favorite features**

The Mighty Micro House features great use of bright colors and open space (helped by the dormers in the loft). Curtained cabinets, such as the ones under the sink, are a great technique to cover the clutter within. They take up almost no space and weight; can easily be changed out when a new look, color, or style is desired; and, most importantly, don't eat up "swing space" — you just push them aside to gain access to the stored goods. Oh yeah, they also cost far less than cabinet doors and are far easier to install!

# THE PROFESSOR'S POD

**Deek Diedricksen**

**28 square feet**

**New Jersey**

**A**NOTHER ONE of this book's tiniest structures, the Professor's Pod was an exercise in building from recycled and salvaged materials. The client, an NYU sociology professor, approached me out of the blue, looking to buy one of my original cabins, the Hickshaw. Dragging this shelter out of the Vermont woods during mud season proved difficult, however, so we struck a deal to build him a newer, better, and "bigger" structure. This pod on wheels can be rolled by two people and now resides by a pond near a vacation cabin in the woods of New Jersey. It's an escape in which to read, grade papers, and relax.

With a front wall that opens up for fresh air and a view, a large awning-style window (found on the side of the road), and recycled flooring, the Professor's Pod is certainly a budget build. Especially eye-grabbing is its rear "wild wall" made up of scrap wood cut into 13-inch segments. This technique allowed me to cut back on material costs, use what would otherwise have ended up in a landfill, and give this simple and boxy structure a kick of visual fun.

The wild wall, while
more time-consuming
to build than a wall
made of plywood
sheathing, has
worked well for me
in many cases. It's
also just entertain-
ing to put one of
these walls together
and watch a pile of
junky scrap wood
become a mosaic art
piece. In addition,
the Professor's Pod
marked the first time
I ever used smoky-
colored Tuftex poly-
carbonate roofing
(for the front wall),
and I'm glad I did.
This tinted material
offers a little privacy
but also allows in
some natural light
while not overdoing it.
A solar-cooked NYU
professor isn't what
I was going for.

# THE GYPSY JUNKER

Deek Diedricksen

28 square feet

Framingham, Massachusetts

**W**HILE NOT NECESSARILY my favorite structure, the Gypsy Junker is probably the one that's gotten me the most media attention over the years, including a three-page Home and Garden cover story in the *New York Times*.

This project started as a challenge to myself. Could I construct a microcosm of a dwelling using almost nothing but junk found roadside? The Gypsy Junker is named for its slight resemblance to a gypsy wagon and is, in fact, made of junk. It was built over several months as I hunted and pecked for build-worthy goods. Truth be told, I never really "looked" for stuff or went out of my way for any of these pieces; I just happened upon them when en route to places I was headed anyway. With wine-bottle microwindows, flooring scraps, freebie windows, forklift-pallet siding, and even a washing-machine side panel as an outdoor table, the Gypsy Junker was a fun exercise in seeing what could be done with "scrap 'n' crap."

This cabin was intended as a weekend camp cabin (my son's very first campout was in this little shack) or a backyard office (where I worked on some designs). I used it on my YouTube channel as a video tutorial on what could be done with absolute junk. While the project was partly a commentary on excessive wastefulness in the US, I was also attempting to urge people to take several ideas from this build and run with them, and perhaps try them out on a larger scale. Since the launch of the video tour, several Gypsy Junker–like cabins have been constructed around the world.

To fund future builds and videos, and to clear out space on my limited chunk of land outside Boston, I ended up selling this hut — in what became a bidding war — to a very talented and established graphic designer from the greater Boston area. It couldn't have found a better home.

I feel the desk/bed two-in-one works particularly well in the Gypsy Junker. The bed, "long enough for Shaquille O'Neal," as I joke in the video tour, was set at a height comfortable for desk use, complete with a large window. I also love the use of clear polycarbonate roofing. It brings so much needed light into this tiny space; it's easy to install, lightweight, affordable, and durable; and it lets the occupant view the tree limbs swinging in the wind, right overhead.

# HENRIETTA

**A** **MICRO-OFFICE** and a nap nook on wheels, Mimi Day's Henrietta was inspired by my own Gypsy Junker cabin and Tiny Yellow House series on YouTube. It's little more than a closet on wheels but has lots of character and coziness. While it might be a tight fit for those of larger stature, it works very well for its owner. One of the smallest structures in this book, at 4 x 6 feet, it sits atop a mail-order yard trailer (one that supports well over 1,000 pounds) but is still long enough that Mimi can sleep on its cushioned floor. Best yet, when Mimi tires of Henrietta's location and seeks out a new vista or the shade of a tree in the summer heat, she simply hooks this tiny slumber shack to her riding lawnmower and drags it elsewhere. Being on wheels,

Mimi Day

24 square feet

Virginia

it's not a "permanent structure," either, so something like this could be built almost anywhere, without town or county permission.

This little structure is not a house (many of the structures in this book aren't, at least not in a traditional sense). But a hot plate, coffeemaker, and toaster oven could be shoe-horned into this mobile room without much difficulty. I suppose, given the reasonable price to build something like this, that one could also build another to serve as a kitchen, and yet another as a bathroom with a toilet and shower. You could have a whole little wagon train of moveable dwelling units, scattered across a picturesque plot of land — all mobile and all on a small budget.

Built on top of a cheap yard trailer

**favorite features**

I love that the Henrietta is built atop such an affordable yet durable yard trailer. Brand new, it was reasonably priced at around $200. I just might be inspired to try it in the future. The large window is great too. Imagine orienting this toward a lake or a mountain vista. The natural light in here could be dang magnificent. And this is another microhut that could be lifted or assembled on a tree plat-form, easily. A deck surrounded by railings, an Adirondack chair or two, and you're enjoying life, a book, or the sun, up among the birds.

# JEAN'S GYPSY WAGON

Jean Marc
Labrosse

70 (or so)
square feet

Seattle,
Washington

**T**HIS GYPSY-WAGONESQUE inn was dreamed up by Jean Marc Labrosse and hosts guests in the Seattle area. The project took a little over a year to contemplate and complete and was built entirely in Jean's city driveway — the beauty of small structures!

"We wanted to create a low-tech trailer made from sustainable materials," says Jean. "No plastics were used anywhere in this build." The wagon is 10 feet long and 7 feet 8 inches in diameter with a 3-foot tongue; the curved walls help it feel less tiny. With a queen-size bed on the upper platform and a smaller kid space below, there is room inside to sleep a small family.

Top bunk

**favorite features**

Jean's Gypsy Wagon is such a simple yet sophisticated structure, and I mean that with the utmost respect. The outside, with its ornate homemade windows and bright color, seems to set the stage for something fancier, but once inside you're greeted with a more natural, rustic feel — and it's no disappointment. The double-level sleep platforms are great for such a small space and make it possible to sleep two adults and two kids. Not bad for something so darn small!

Jean estimates that this little cabin weighs a ton or so — too heavy to tow on the trailer it was built on — even though it was originally intended for camping. "My need to use every bit of my wood supply got me in trouble," he says. "There also was the worry that during transport a rock would fly up and break our beautiful homemade stained-glass windows, so we ultimately decided to ground it at home in the garden." When they later decided to list it on airbnb. com, there was a flurry of activity. "Not only has the structure paid for itself, but it's afforded us the luxury of being able to go on a few vacations."

Bottom bunk

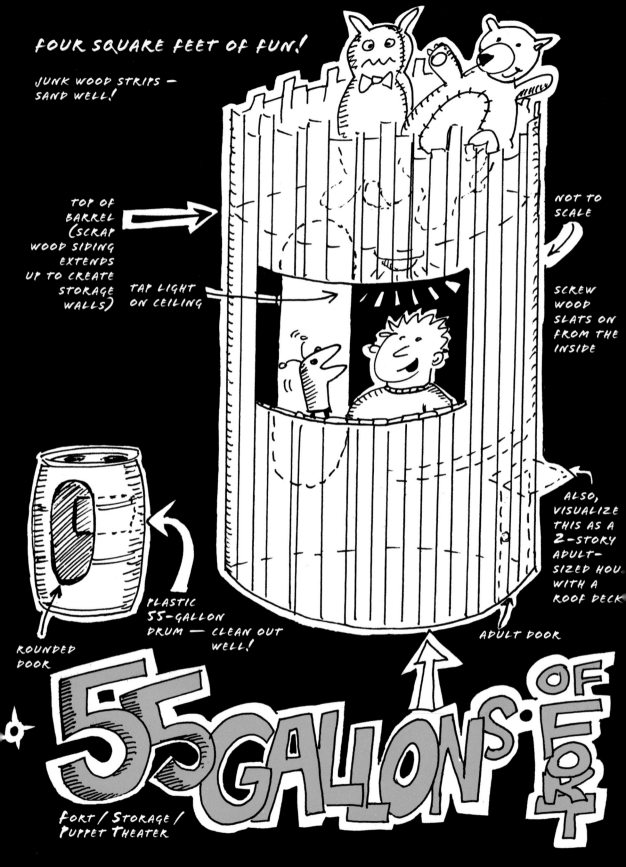

# play-houses & nooks

# 5

**JUST WHEN YOU THOUGHT** we couldn't go any smaller, we've gone and greased up your sides so we can shove you into the realm of the very tiniest of tiny spaces: playhouses and nooks. By this we mean clubhouses, forts, hideouts, and any related supersmall spaces. When you think about it, these little lairs are in many ways fledgling versions of tiny houses, and as whimsical and micro as they may be, one shouldn't be too hasty to write them off as pointless and childish. In both design and decor, there is quite a bit that can be learned and gleaned from these petite places, even when they are built by kids themselves.

# THE LI'L ORANGE PLAYHOUSE

Joel Henriques

24 square feet

Portland, Oregon

**J**OEL HENRIQUES, a talented artist, blogger, and father of two, lives in the realm of the ultra-colorful. Joel also seems to have a penchant for modern design, and it shows in this clubhouse that he drafted and built.

Sitting atop a single sheet of plywood, framed with mere 2x2s, this very simple and straightforward fort is enhanced by the use of bold orange, its lack of clutter, and the well-chosen pendant lamp as the focal piece of the room. If you're going to keep things sparse and minimal you should make your few decor and furniture items count, and Joel clearly knows this. The chalkboard-paint walls (dual functionality at work), electricity (provided by a simple extension cord), and the rather nice homemade Plexiglas windows all show that Joel put some thought into this little playhouse, but at the same time knew to not overthink it.

The Li'l Orange Playhouse is a tiny little space, but inviting with its colors — a palette that might brighten up the rain-heavy region the designer lives in. This thing would be amazing perched in a tree with a little deck, not that it's at all shabby in its ground-bound form. (I keep mentioning the tree house–conversion potential of many of these structures, but that's only because with microstructures it's such a simple transition.) Either way, forget the kids; I'd like to spend a night in this thing, or maybe build one just a little larger and plop it deep in the woods, streamside, lit by lanterns, and accessible only by a long, meandering, scenic trail.

# THE BOOK NOOK

**Deek Diedricksen**

**18 square feet**

**New York, New York**

**A** **SHELTER** (or pod, as I like to call it) on wheels that's small enough to squeeze through most any household door? Why not? If artist Piet Mondrian commissioned a microshack — a simple indoor kid fort or adult reading escape — this might be it. It's simple but modern, it's budget-friendly, and it takes in a heck of a lot of natural light. After all, it's a space designed for hiding out and reading. The clear front wall showcases a spontaneous array of stud framing while also providing a glimpse of some custom mural artwork (spray paint and thick Sharpie markers) on the back wall.

This little project came together via a kind of spree I like to call *Operation Use It Up*: I grab whatever leftover wood and roofing pieces I have and put them to work with a mix of new materials to round things out. At only 34 inches wide and 6 feet long, the Book Nook is extremely tiny but still big enough to contain most adults and serve as an indoor or outdoor getaway.

The stud work of the front wall provides an attachment surface for the see-through Tuftex paneling, and the wider horizontal pieces, 2x4s, also double as shelving. Whatever is displayed on these mini shelves also makes interesting silhouettes when the Book Nook is lighted from within. The 10-inch-wide tongue-and-groove planks I used for siding worked well too. These boards are sturdy and make for quick coverage over any structure's frame.

# THE NISKER NOOK

**Morten Nisker Toppenberg**

**16 square feet**

**Finland**

**M** **ORTEN NISKER E-MAILED ME** with these photos as a thank-you for the inspiration from my blog, and I was taken with the overall fun vibe of this little play shack. It is, more or less, a deck-top shed in micro form, with a clean little table inside, some minimal yet effective wall decor and storage, and a few windows. Nothing more. Yet somehow it works. Again, there's something to be said for simplicity.

I might have painted the Nisker Nook's back wall a golf-grass green, except for the stud work, but even without painting the inside, Morten has succeeded in creating a light, spacious atmosphere in only 16 square feet. I love the little picnic-style bench as well. The beauty of such simply shaped and sized shacks (say *that* 10 times fast!) is that later, when the kids outgrow them, they can be used as tiny sheds for deck storage. I'm a big fan of structures with more than one potential use, or with the possibility of future "transformative" uses.

# THE LITTLE BLUE BUMP

**Deek Diedricksen**

**24 square feet**

**Boston, Massachusetts**

**T**RUTH BE TOLD, I was never a huge fan of the Little Blue Bump microcabin, but its video is among my most popular, and the cabin has been rebuilt by others around the globe more than any other design of mine. This is probably due to how easy, cheap, and quick a "wooden tent" like this is to build.

Basically, the floor is one thick piece of plywood raised a bit off the ground, and its two ends are made from similar stock, only rounded off with a jigsaw. Add in some recycled-junk windows, a clear polycarbonate roof, and you start to see the old Deek-design pattern here: build less, with less, for less, in less time . . . and make sure it gets *a lot* of natural light. The cabin later sold and has been relocated, but video viewers continue to build their own, and I can't say that this bums me out at all.

I like the Little Blue Bump's little cantilevered window. It bumps out one part of the cabin almost a whole foot, serves as a shelf, and adds some aesthetic variety to an otherwise boring cabin wall. Also, the flooring is just cheap, lauan paneling, which worked far better than I could have imagined!

Windows made from pot lid and water jug

# THE CRATE ESCAPE

Deek Diedricksen

12 square feet

Stoughton, Massachusetts

**T**WELVE SQUARE FEET, DEEK? *You must not be firing on all cylinders! You're inhaling too much of that particleboard sawdust!* The birth of this box began with just that: a box. When my neighbor, wild man Paul LaCivita, brought me an enormous, overbuilt shipping crate he had found (it took two of us to move it), I immediately envisioned an unassuming little cube sitting in a field or any other scenic locale in which an occupant could curl up, perhaps with a good book, and just relax. Rocket science? No. Spacious? Definitely not. Fun? I certainly think so . . . But then again, I probably do have a bit of sawdust on the brain.

**favorite features**

Yes, it's just a box, but the Crate Escape makes for an unusual, intimate space with a great deal of natural light because of the translucent front wall. This wall swings open, and for airflow in warmer weather, a simple, rolled-up drop-screen could be installed. The cantilevered window box makes this cube feel a hair bigger than it is and also serves as shelf space. Both the back wall and the floor are clad in antique, freebie tongue-and-groove lumber from the same lot that supplied flooring for the Bread Box (page 94). The rear wall, I might add, is cedar, making this little book box smell great. As for the tiny "peek window," it's the lid to an IKEA storage container — a window with trim, all in one piece, for about $3.99. I've used these lids countless times in kid forts and sheds. I just use a jigsaw to cut an opening in the wall that's slightly smaller than the container, then sand the wood edges. I drill two pilot holes in the frame of the container to avoid splitting it. Once attached, I seal around the perimeter with silicone caulk.

TOOLS
MATE

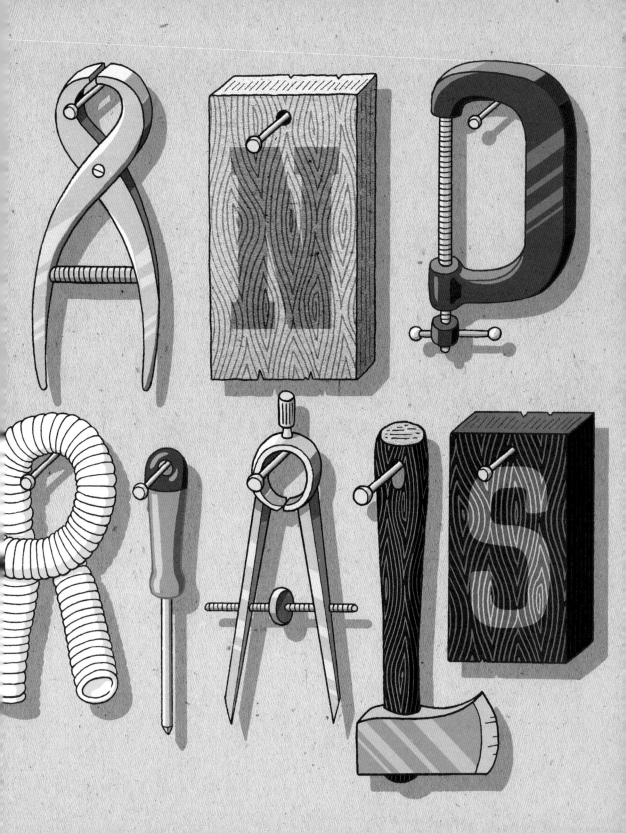

# gathering your tools

**6**

**NOW THAT YOU'VE DILIGENTLY STUDIED** the preceding onslaught of microshelters in every size, shape, and form, perhaps you're beginning to develop a growing case of cabin envy, or at least you've found some sources of inspiration. If so, then it's time to grab your rusty, dusty old tool box and hop to it!

You won't find an extensive primer on tools here, or the exciting history of pliers, or any lengthy segments on how *not* to hold a punch awl (the point faces down, for the record). After all, there is already a forest-devastating amount of tool and technique introduction books out there — and most of them are about as exciting as watching mold race. That said, I do want to recommend a few relatively uncommon tools that I have found particularly valuable, reliable, and affordable. All of these are hand tools, which offer two notable advantages: peace and quiet.

Most of the work I do tends to be outdoors, frequently in off-grid locales. I could lug in a generator, but that would mean storing and maintaining an expensive, backbreaking-to-haul "beast box." Plus, a generator guzzles gas, which I'd also have to pay for and carry into the woods. I, for one, love to hear a stream gurgle, a cricket chirp, or a porcupine pass wind while I'm working out in the woods. Fire up a generator, though, and it's Goodbye, Nature! (Remember the scene in *Bambi* where all the animals are fleeing the wildfire? Well, you've pretty much created a sonic version of that.) I'm not anti-generator or against power tools by any means, but I like to at least have the option of using something like a brace and bit where appropriate. Besides, you just might find a new favorite tool for your toolbox!

# BRACE AND BIT

**THE BRACE AND BIT'S** an oldie and goodie but unfortunately is not widely sold anymore. Ask most young hardware store employees on what aisle a brace and bit might be found and you're bound to get a "this guy looks like he's lost his mind and indulges in rubber cement sculpting" look. (Believe me, I've gotten that look — but, to be fair, I also enjoy a good glue-sculpting session.)

You might remember your grandfather owning one of these, or you may have come across them in shop class back in your middle school

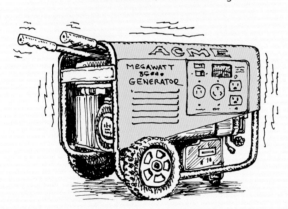

## Tiny Words of Wisdom ON STRUCTURE AND DESIGN

We want to create a sense of openness in small-space designs, yet we recognize that divisions add function, privacy, and a sense of structure. If interior walls are not load-bearing, as is the case with most small cabins and tiny homes on trailers, you have some flexibility. You can minimize wall thickness and frame skinny walls with 2x3 or 2x2 support lumber and still have a strong enough wall to hold your final surface. In some cases you can use just the ¾-inch plywood itself and save even more interior room.

— **PEPPER CLARK**, *owner of the design/blog/build company Bungalow to Go*

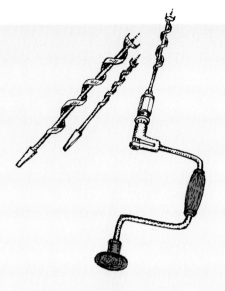

concrete wall. Try that with a modern plastic-housed power tool and you'll soon be asking the janitorial staff for a dustpan, but with the brace and bit, the only damage you're bound to inflict is to the wall. (Be mindful, I might add, not to throw it against drywall — the results, while fun to watch, could be costly and, again, require that dustpan.)

days. I'm particularly fond of this tool. For one thing, I find them so cheaply online and at thrift shops that I can rarely pass them up. I own seven or eight. I'm a brace-and-bit hoarder, I suppose. On eBay, I bought a set of two, with an assortment of bits, for only eight bucks, including shipping.

The brace and bit uses a combination of simple physical pressure and a corkscrew motion to drill holes. It's also one heck of a heavy-duty and sturdy implement. To demonstrate this at workshops or speaking engagements, I've taken one of these beauties and thrown it against a

# BLOCK PLANE

**ANOTHER NIFTY HAND TOOL** is the block plane. I'll admit I don't use this as much as some other tools, but they're easy to come by cheap (used), and it can't hurt to keep one in your arsenal. BPs, as they're known in the hip-hop community (not true at all), are hand-driven, inclined "shavers" in the simplest sense. You want a door trimmed just a hair so that it doesn't stick in the summer? Well, just bust out the old block plane. In many cases you won't have to remove

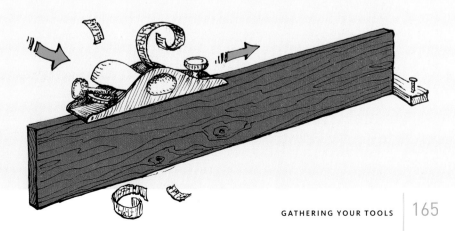

the door to get the job done, and it's not nearly as messy, noisy, or lung-irritating as using a power sander. It's also more gradual and precise than buzzing through the door's edge with a circular saw (another tool you do want to have, by the way). There are many sizes and varieties of block planes, each particularly tuned for different material-removal work, and there are bench planes for end grain work too, so don't neglect to ask a few questions or do a little research before grabbing one for whatever job might be at hand.

These little guys, some not so little, are also great for shaving down the edges of woodworking projects or cutting down the edges of melamine edge tape (fake laminate end-grain strips) on plywood builds. A block plane also makes for a rather handsome-looking paperweight, should you ever have to retire one. But the beauty here is that these tools, aside from the blade that will need sharpening from time to time, are nearly indestructible. (Note: I wouldn't throw these against a wall, though, as they're instruments of precision.)

# UTILITY KNIFE, aka BOX CUTTER

**WHAT BETTER WAY** to ensure that grizzly bears, zombies, and door-to-door vacuum cleaner salesmen are kept at bay than to have a box cutter on hand at all times? Kidding! These are handy as heck, though, and they take up almost no space. They're also very, very sharp — so be careful, and do not leave them lying unattended within the grasp of children. Always be sure to retract the blade when not in use.

Basically, any time you need to give some wood a quick shave, unbind plastic-strapped lumber, cut or trim thin wood or asphalt shingles, slice the tip off a tube of caulk, score Plexiglas for a break, or even crudely chisel out a recess for a door's lock set, this tool's going to pay for itself a hundred times over. And what's a utility knife cost, five dollars? Six, I hear, if you get the one that's bedazzled with faux rhinestones.

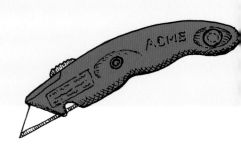

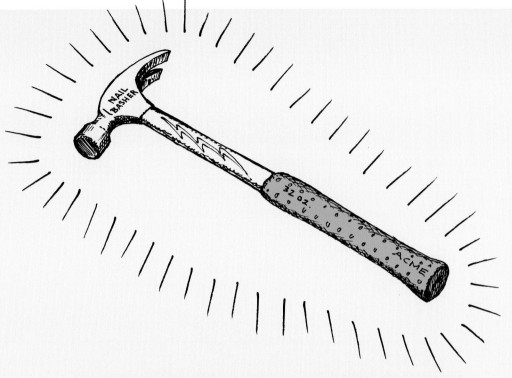

# HAMMERS (or THE DEEK VS. DUSTIN DEBATE)

**WHAT PERSON WHO** plans on building anything isn't going to have a hammer? It would be like going to the beach without a swimsuit, or baking a cake without an oven. I know it seems ridiculous to even bother to include such a rudimentary tool here, but I've chosen to do so because of what I dub, in speaking appearances, the *Deek vs. Dustin Debate.*

Dustin, my brother, is from the school that says you need to have the best state-of-the-art hammer that's offered. Not only can it drive a nail, it also has a built-in cell phone, a pinwheel, a barometer, a bicycle pump, and it's hollow and insulated to hold your favorite post-job beverage — that is, when it's not being used as a makeshift saxophone. Dustin is very good at what he does in carpentry, and I can't argue that going all-out with a top-notch hammer, or any tool, is going to hurt your chances of a job well done, but I'm from a rather different plane of thought. The hammers I own are, by comparison, junk. Since I organize and host many workshops, I can't justify spending a ton of money on hammers that might go missing or be abused (not that you can hurt a hammer so easily). I own, easily, a dozen or so hammers, and a good majority were yanked from yard sales. An old, slightly rusty hammer will perform just as well as a shiny new one and should last quite a long time. So why spend on a hammer that is fancier than your needs?

The one word of caution I'll offer is against wooden-handled hammers. You'll find these in all the hardware stores and will be tempted by their low price, but while they do a good job of absorbing the shock of each blow, over time the handles tend to get loosened from the head, and this can be dangerous. Someday that hammer head will fly off, and I really wouldn't want to be in its path. So, if given the choice, I'd pick a metal-rubberized or fiberglass-handled model. To each his own, though. Wooden handles *can* be tightened and affixed to their heads again, but most people neglect to do so, or do it improperly. There are also many types of hammers —

waffle-headed ones, ball-peen hammers, tack hammers, M. C. Hammers, and the list goes on and on — but for starters, a simple claw hammer will do.

I might add that Dustin, sick of my old beaten and ugly tools, eventually gifted me a really nice, magnetic-headed framing hammer, one so large that it could stop a bull ele-phant dead in its tracks with a single swing. I do love the thing, and refer to it as the "Hammer of Thor," but for the most part it's just too big and long for repeat use and good control. Honestly, I mainly use it for demoli-tion. So therein lies another tip: Don't get overly macho and buy the biggest, heaviest hammer you can get your mitts on — you might be swinging that thing thousands of times in a sin-gle day. Unless you *are* Thor, just take it easy. Pick a hammer that is com-fortable for you. I prefer a 16-ounce hammer myself, and nothing more.

**Tiny Words of Wisdom ON SHELVING**

There never seems to be enough room in the bathroom, so it's really important to be as efficient as possible here. For us that means taking advantage of the space above the toilet, and not just by adding shelves. What you really need is a work surface. So in our homes we build a shelving unit that has a door that folds down and stops 90 degrees to the wall. This creates a counter space and reveals shelving as well as a mirror when open (it also hides your mess when closed). It's the perfect spot to make sure you look your best!

— **DAN LOUCHE,** *tiny-house designer/builder at tinyhomebuilders.com*

# BUCKETS

**A BUCKET IS LIKE** the neglected distant cousin of the family: you forget to send them the Christmas card, you never know their birthday, and you seldom pay them any attention, but when you do, you realize, "Wow, I've taken this really cool, interesting person for granted — I'm such a heel!" The many uses of buckets are often overlooked. I make sure to keep a few on hand for a variety of reasons. In addition to the usual functions of transporting materials and bailing water, here are a few things these suckers can be used for:

- Mixing tub for mortar or concrete

- Low sawhorses (two buckets flipped upside down)

- Tool tote (you can even buy a tool-sorting sleeve that fits right inside a standard 5-gallon bucket)

- Street drumming to make extra cash for your project (kidding, sort of — I actually used to do this back in the day)

- Makeshift seat (they make padded attachments for this!)

- Single-step ladder (just don't stack them — you'll get hurt)

- Cooler for drinks (just fill with ice)

- Emergency toilet or permanent composting toilet (there are several books on this subject, including *The Humanure Handbook*, by Joseph Jenkins, and *The Water-Wise Home*, by Laura Allen)

- Form for making concrete footings or large concrete flowerpots

- Backwoods rain collector (with help from a strung-up tarp funneling into the bucket)

- Budget-friendly Halloween mask (just drill holes)? Nah . . .

- Vessel for washing clothes in (while off-grid, camping, on the road)

And I'm sure there are *plenty* more uses! You get the idea.

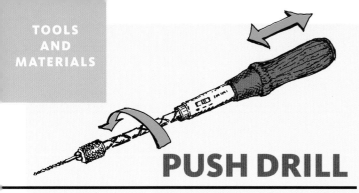

# PUSH DRILL

# UNIVERSAL DEMOLITION TOOL

**I DON'T SEE** push drills available at stores anymore, but I know you can buy them through antique tool dealers online. The two I own are from, you guessed it, a yard sale and a flea market. These small tools are just what the name implies. Think of a screwdriver that can receive not only Phillips or common screwdriver bits but also regular drill bits. Pushing the handle downward turns the head that holds the bit. At the end of the stroke you release the pressure and the handle springs back up, ready for the next push. If a pogo stick and a screwdriver had kids, this would be the result.

The push drill is small and compact, and it has saved my wrists from hand-turn work in a few off-grid locations where my drill batteries ran out and I had no means or time to juice 'em up again. Quiet, small, and light, it's a good hardware-removal tool to have around if you're going to be scrounging wood, hardware, and furnishings for your build. Since these drills are designed for small bits and, therefore, smaller work, pairing one of these with a bulkier brace and bit might be a good idea.

**THE UDT** ain't nothin' to mess with! That sounds like something you might see scrawled on a bathroom wall in a dive bar. It's true, though; this is one tough tool. If you're taking the salvaging approach when building your dream shack, tree house, or grand bell-'n'-whistle-laden cabin, you just might want to have this tool in your arsenal. Why? Well, aside from having a built-in hammer head, it can pull nails, pry apart boards, and tear down walls and framing with a 2-inch-wide demolition claw. Should you accidentally drop the tool on your foot, you'll find it's also efficient at removing toenails . . .

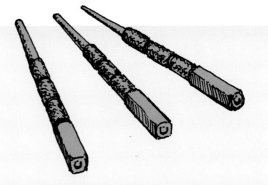

# NAIL SET

**ANOTHER COMMONLY** overlooked mini tool, the nail set or nail punch (or just plain "setter") is worth its weight in gold (which isn't saying much, I suppose, as it's so tiny). This simple "dollar tool" is used with a hammer to drive nail heads flush with or slightly recessed into wood, after you've driven the nails just so far with a hammer alone. This preserves the aesthetics of the project, since trying to overdrive a nail results in striking and denting the wood.

Nail sets come in a few different sizes; ideally, the point of the nail set is just slightly smaller than the head of the nail you're driving. If the nail set is bigger than the head, it'll make a bigger hole than the nail, which defeats the whole purpose of masking the nail. Typically, nail sets are used with finish nails, which have small, smooth heads designed for setting, but you can use the tool for other types of nails and other fasteners.

Sure, in some builds you don't want to hide the honesty of the construction and might choose to leave nail heads exposed — I often do — but if finer trim or cabinetwork is in order, a nail setter's going to be your friend. In a pinch, these can also be used as a blunt punch awl to make a guide hole for a screw or drill bit, and I've even seen people use them as bottle openers (like I said, worth their weight in gold).

If you're really out of luck, a 16-penny nail can be used as a nail set, but it takes a steadier hand to make it work, and the nail will only last for so long before it begins to bend.

**Tiny Words of Wisdom ON STRUCTURE AND DESIGN**

Want a mini kitchen or a fridge to fit in a small space? Cantilever it outside your room and you'll use no floor space. A bump-out is basically a box with another roof outside your main structure. You may not even need a roof for a small one that is under your eaves. Small bump-outs are easy; bigger ones may require a foundation and some further construction know-how.

**— JOSEPH EBSWORTH**, *tiny-cabin owner/builder, blogger at SolarBurrito.com*

# DEEK 'N' DUSTIN SPEAK

If you build enough with the same person or crew, you're eventually bound to develop your own slang or verbal shorthand. So, just for kicks, here's a guide to some of the loco lingo that my brother, Dustin, and I toss around on the job site. The two of us have worked together for well over a decade on countless cabins, tree houses, home improvement projects, and beyond, so it's only natural that we've developed our own work-site gibberish over the years.

**BASHER:** An overzealous hammer-wielder who hits and dents the wood more often than the nail head.

## BEAST BOX:

A generator (usually a loud one).

**SHOFFICE:** A shed converted into an office.

## BOOM STICK:

A hammer (usually a large one).

**CLOFFICE:** A closet that's been transformed into a mini home office. Or, just a supertiny closet-like cabin, often in a backyard, that's being used as an office or small studio.

**GTG:** GOOD TO GO. WE'RE/ IT'S DONE.

**GIVE IT THE MILO TOUCH:** To come up with a fix or approach that's more utilitarian than aesthetically pleasing but is clever in its own right. Named in honor of a friend.

**GROUNDBOUND:** Describes a dwelling built on or attached to the ground, as opposed to a tiny house or cabin on wheels, or one on a trailer.

**FUTZ IT:** Just "cheat it," or give it a quick fix and get it done (don't dwell on it too long).

# PUT SOME LIPSTICK ON IT:

Use a technique or means to make some ugly aspect of a project less unattractive, often in a quick and affordable manner.

## SEND IT HOME:

Used when you're holding a board in place and waiting for your helper to fasten it. For example, when I've got a piece set and it's ready to be screwed or nailed, I'd tell my brother to "send it home," meaning we're good; drive the nail.

## HEALTH:
A slang measurement term to convey a length just over a certain distance. The opposite of *ill* measurements.

## ILL:
Used in measuring to convey that something is just a hair under a certain length, as in "Dustin, I need a board 38 ill" (just under 38 inches). It's easier than saying "thirty-seven and fifteen-sixteenths."

# STICK WITH BUBBLES: A level.

## SCRAPPER:

A person who cruises the streets on trash day looking for large metal items to sell to a scrap metal recycler. Scrappers often advertise with classified titles like "Will haul away your junk metal for free!" Some of these guys really know what they're doing and make some good coin on it too.

## PLB:

The quick and affordable decorating approach of using pillows, lanterns, and books. (See "Decor on a Dime," page 191).

## SLOP TRIM:

Quick and cheap trim that looks decent enough but not fancy.

## SEAGULL:

An individual at scrap yards and salvage depots who combs around for little items here and there, often aggravating the yard owner by using up his/her time in exchange for little money made. However, some scrap and recycling yards welcome seagulls with open arms because their purchases can add up over time.

## SHIP IT:

Shorthand for "It's done. Let's get on to the next thing."

Art made with scraps and leftover paints

Shelving made from free wood

Salad-bowl pendant light

Free roadside windows

Bench made of recycled flooring

# budgeting & salvaging

**7**

**SO MANY PEOPLE ASK ME,** "Deek, how the heck do you come across all your free building materials? I mean, how can you build so affordably? Wizardry? Black magic? A pact with some eight-armed, underworld demigod of refuse?"

Nope. It's nothing so difficult, nor soul-sacrificing. Step one is just to think outside the box. Following are five simple tips that can save you a tidy sum. Keep in mind that none of these ideas are going to work for everyone stylistically, but they all work without sacrificing quality or strength in a build, and they help lessen that "Oh, crap; a tiny house (or shed or studio) is going to cost me *x* grand?!" gut punch.

Remember, every penny counts. . . . Speaking of which, you can tile a floor with pennies and epoxy, and it looks absolutely *amazing*!

# TIPS FOR THE TINY BUDGET

**1. SUBFLOOR AND FLOORING IN ONE:** Instead of the conventional approach of using junky, off-gassing oriented strandboard (OSB) for subflooring and topping it with a standard flooring material, you can use a high-quality, and nicer-looking, plywood instead. Yes, cabinet-grade birch or poplar, for example, costs more than OSB, which may seem counter to my own advice, but this subfloor is going to look so nice it can stay as is, without another layer of flooring (such as expensive tongue-and-groove hardwoods). This will not only save you money, but also time — which, they say, is money after all. A few quick coats of polyurethane will make this floor shine, and down the road, should it get beat or you tire of the look, just pick up where you left off and install that upper layer of flooring. Also, with only one layer of flooring, you're freeing up ¾ inch of interior height without affecting the overall height of the structure. This can be particularly helpful when you're building a tiny home on a trailer and have to conform to Department of Transportation restrictions (no more than 13 feet 6 inches tall, total). Every inch or fraction thereof counts in so small a structure. Mark my words. And yes, if you want to save even more money, and are fine with a very rough and rustic look, you can use lower-grade AC fir plywood — it's just as strong, and works rather well.

**2. DON'T OVERLOOK THE SMALL THINGS.** So you're driving around doing errands and your spider-sense catches a few doors sitting on the side of the road. Upon second glance you quickly see that they're lousy, cheap, hollow-core doors — not the kind that will do you any good in most cases. But,

**Tiny Words of Wisdom ON DUAL FUNCTIONALITY**

One thing we have come to understand about efficiency in a small space is this: everything needs more than one purpose. A bench can be much more than simple seating; it could also serve as extra sleeping and storage space. A wall-mounted table could function as a personal workspace during the day and a dinner table at night (and can be dropped down and out of the way when not in use). Use any small cracks behind or in between items for extra hiding space. For example, the space between your counter and fridge might just be enough to slide a folding chair into, giving you extra seating when needed. By having more than one function, things use up less space in already tight quarters, while at the same time utilizing that space more efficiently.

— **CHRISTOPHER AND MALISSA TACK,** *tiny-house builders/owners and bloggers at chrisandmalissa.com*

Tiny Words of Wisdom
## ON STRUCTURE AND DESIGN

Consider using the mathematical patterns that we find in nature to inspire functional yet organic designs that can be applied to storage, windows, doors, trim, and more. The golden ratio, fractals, and repeating geometric designs help give your space unity and peace. Tangrams and other simple shape-combination games can spark your imagination when you come up against designer's block.

— **JOE COOVER**, *tiny-house dweller, blogger at LongStoryShortHouse.com*

as you're now a further-educated, savvy, uber-creative, and thrifty individual (all because you picked up this book!), you zoom in a little more and realize that these cruddy doors are bedecked with 3-inch door hinges, coat hooks, and all sorts of cabinetry pulls, lock sets, or slide bolts. Bam! In the span of 10 minutes, with a screwdriver from your road kit (page 181), you remove these items, thus saving them from a landfill and, better yet, from your future "to purchase" list. You can also sell what you don't use if you end up acquiring a lot of hardware over time. Old, classic doorknobs are another thing to keep an eye out for, some being worth a decent chunk o' change. I've seen prices around $80 for a single vintage knob. (See page 186 for more tips on salvaging.)

3. **FURRING STRIPS FOR TRIM.** If you're content with a simple, less frilly look, you can use furring strips (the cheap 8-foot-long strapping boards you can buy for about $1.69 each at lumberyards) to make your own window, door, and/or wall trim rather easily. No, it won't look like Victorian crown molding, and it won't give your home any semblance of Taj Mahal grandeur, but I've used this method many times and always been pleased with the look — and even more pleased with the savings. I've never had a client complain, either. If you need to neaten up or thin down the stock, a

**BUDGETING AND SALVAGING**

My assorted pile of lumber leftovers might not be organized, but it's all in one area, which for me is *really* organized, and very helpful in times of need. The "scraps of scraps" often later go to my kids for their forts, or are painted and drawn on and sold as salvaged artwork online.

quick trip through a table saw or planer will take care of things. A router table can do wonders too, by etching curves and layers into your stock. But I usually keep things on the simple side. In most cases, I just pick through the pile for the very best boards and use them as they are or with a nice coat of stain to bring out the wood grain. A time- and mess-saving tip: prepaint or stain these thin boards *before* you install them.

**4. SAVE YOUR SCRAPS.** This is a "finding what you already have" tip. Hear me out. Yes, a clean job site is important, but it's still possible to maintain order while saving your scraps — just put them in a designated area to keep things less chaotic. I do understand that some of you out there are neat freaks and might obsess about immediately removing any waste and clutter from the building scene, but try to resist! Here's why: You're framing a wall and need just a piece of blocking or some angled knee braces, but you're fresh out of lumber.

Well, a trip to the lumber store for such a little piece (or three or four) is going to kill your momentum, cost you a bit extra, waste your time and energy, and just be an overall pain. *But fear not!* You most likely already have those very pieces you need right in that scrap pile — the one you've been dying to burn, donate to the kids' fort fund, or throw away. So resist that urge to toss it all! At least for a little while. When this tip does in fact save you a tiny bit of what remains of your sanity, feel free to lavish any thank-you gifts upon me.

**5. SECONDHAND WINDOWS AND DOORS.** There are some incredible character-loaded cast-offs waiting for you out there on Craigslist, in Habitat for Humanity ReStores, at yard sales and architectural salvage yards, in newspaper classifieds, at transfer stations (a.k.a. the town dump), etc., not to mention those found through old-fashioned word of mouth. You may not get the exact size and quantity of doors or windows you were looking for, but if you're able to remain flexible, you might end up with a unique look that's even better than what you had inked out. On the other hand, if you're patient, you'll most likely find just what you need, without compromise.

# LET THE FREE JUNK LEAD

I often let the material dictate the build. I'm not saying that you should base the look of your home around a single unbelievable door, but I wouldn't write off the idea completely. I found a free window a while back — a 4 x 8-foot sucker, just monstrous, 32 panes in all — and ever since then I've been madly sketching lanternlike tree houses, all based around the use of this single window. The window becomes a wall, the wall a focal point, and the rather unusual tree house is then loaded with light. You never know how an unexpected find might inspire you. Don't be afraid to let the free junk lead you. If you're willing to take the chance, you just might be thrilled with the result.

## Tiny Words of Wisdom ON STORAGE

If your tiny house is on a permanent foundation, also consider building a separate storage area. Keep only the items you use daily inside your home, and keep seldom or seasonally used items in the extra storage area outside, which could be as simple as a tiny, unheated shed. Furthermore, the area beneath a tiny house trailer or any raised small structure is seldom seen as a place for usable storage. Get yourself lockable plastic bins to hold large or bulky items to slide in and out as needed. The tiny house overhead will help protect your bins from the elements.

**—STEVEN HARRELL**, *owner of TinyHouseListings.com*

## SCRAPPY SECRETS:
# BUILDING WITH SALVAGED AND RECYCLED MATERIALS

**BY NOW** you've probably sensed a "subtle" theme that runs throughout my projects and designs: *I like to build things with free junk*. "Curbside culling" is a term I coined a while back, and it covers everything from yard-sale searching and word-of-mouth acquisitions to dumpster diving and back-lot browsing, all of which can make a microshelter much more affordable. In addition to the obvious environmental benefits, using recycled goods can make your structure stand out from the pack — in a very good way.

There are, however, some ins, outs, dos, and don'ts of the trade, and I'd like to cover a few of the more common, worthwhile goods you're going to come across when cruising the streets. You don't have to wake up early to race the trash crew for prime pickings, and you don't have to combat fellow "seagulls" (junk hunters) with your fancy moves. Just keep your eyes peeled any time you're on the road. Don't worry, it's not brain surgery; you'll do just fine.

What are you waiting for? Get out there and start some creative harvesting — and enjoy the process, the savings, and the eventual results.

## Windows

These things are strewn everywhere. With increasing technological advances and insulation efficiency (R-value) standards, homeowners are ditching their old (perfectly good) windows at a darn rapid rate. For you and me, this is not a bad thing by any means. I can't tell you the number of windows I've come across, grabbed, and later used in my own projects or just sold to pay for construction items I can't find for free.

There are, however, a few things to be wary of when it comes to windows. Beyond avoiding cracked glass or broken frames (unless the window is *amazing* and could be fixed easily enough), you might want to pass on older windows. Not only are most "antique" windows single-paned, and therefore less efficient, but their glazing (the putty that holds the panes in) often needs work or replacing and can sometimes contain a percentage of asbestos. These windows are more likely to be covered with lead-based sealants and paints, too, both things you don't want to be sprinkling on your breakfast cereal! Now, if the windows are perfectly intact, I'm not saying you can't use them, as I've made use of plenty of them in sheds and shacks,

# ROAD TOOLS

Here's a quick list of tools that I often stash in my vehicle in case I need to do some quick dismantling on the roadside, at a transfer station, or in *your* garage at night! (Kidding . . . kidding . . .) These enable me to take things apart safely and to store them cleanly and securely for transport in my vehicle. If you have a truck or a trailer, you'll be way ahead of the pack and able to haul just about anything you want, but even the smallest of cars will work for most found items (well, maybe not hot tubs, grand pianos, and fridges!).

> Tarp (to keep your vehicle clean)
> Small crowbar/cat's-paw (small, crowbarlike tool designed for pulling nails)
> Hammer
> Utility knife or folding knife
> Tape measure
> Rope
> Goggles
> Bungee cords
> Pliers
> Chisel
> Hand saw
> Bucket (to store odds and ends and small finds)
> Small socket wrench set
> Phillips and flat-head screwdrivers
> Battery-operated power drill (optional, but certainly quick and helpful)
> Gloves

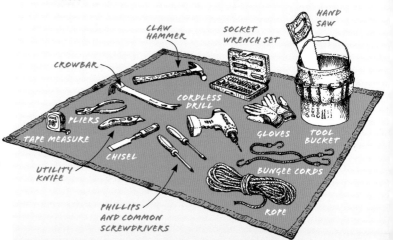

CLAW HAMMER · SOCKET WRENCH SET · HAND SAW · CROWBAR · CORDLESS DRILL · PLIERS · GLOVES · TOOL BUCKET · TAPE MEASURE · CHISEL · UTILITY KNIFE · PHILLIPS AND COMMON SCREWDRIVERS · BUNGEE CORDS · ROPE

but just be careful, especially if it's
an installation that will be in close
proximity to kids, since lead expo-
sure is dangerous for children.

That said, if you ever find any
antique-looking stained-glass
windows, or Gothic-arched
church windows, grab them and
hold on to them for dear life!
They're *very* valuable.

## Doors

Logically, doors would be the next
topic of consideration here, and
they too are abundant. New, they
can be incredibly expensive, so on
any build I've done for a client, if I
can incorporate a nice, vintage door
that actually enhances the look of
the structure while decreasing
my cash outlay, you know darn well
I'm gonna play that hand.

## TO THE NERVOUS AND UNCERTAIN:

One key thing to remember is that most people are thrilled to see that you're taking
these items from their curb. Remind yourself of this if you are wary of approaching any
prime pickings. In this more environmentally aware age, most citizens of Anytown,
USA, or worldwide, will be happy to know that their items, which they might have felt
guilty about tossing to begin with, are finding a new home. Some might even see you
browsing or picking and then come out and offer you goods that they hadn't yet had the
time to haul out. This has happened to me time and time again.

Vintage doors typically are built differently (often better) than most standard stock doors you'll find out there today. Granted, you'll see some amazing new doors with incredibly good R-values, but whether you use them will depend on the caliber, intent, and overall look of your project. For the budget-minded soul, just keep a lookout for replaced doors. Like windows, these are often just sitting curbside, waiting for a new home. At any given time, I seem to have about three or four in stock, which gives me the luxury of options when I'm faced with a need. When my stock gets too thick, I just sell a few.

You can also build your own board-and-batten doors, which is surprisingly easy. The sky's the limit in terms of materials and design: multicolored boards, mixed lumber stock, inset windows or wine-bottle ends, carved designs — you can get as highfalutin and original as you want.

## Hardware

Although small in the overall scheme of a building project, hardware seems to be the most overlooked realm of ever-present freebies out there. I really do mean ever-present. Most people will see a roadside pile of cheap doors and pass them up without a single synapse-fire of consideration. But true scrounger 'n' savers are wiser than that. Take it from a guy

who won't have to buy hinges, hooks, knobs, or drawer pulls for a few decades. Now, you may be thinking this a waste of time and energy — all for items so very small — but aside from the motivation of saving perfectly good metalwork from the landfill, consider that hinges, for example, can run up to three or four dollars each. Now consider that the average home has several doors and swinging cabinet fronts, and you'll start to get a feel for the bigger picture.

I once bought a small box full of old, rusty hinges for two dollars from a barn estate sale in my town. After using many of them, I sold the rest of the lot on eBay for almost $100. Vintage hardware is hard to come by, and it's expensive at "salvage boutiques," so be on the lookout for old doors being tossed. Smashed-up dressers often have nice hardware on them, as do kitchen cabinets, which are frequently updated and are loaded with metallic goodies. Learn to look beyond the initial face value of each item you come across — you'll be amazed at what's left behind.

## Pallet Wood

Pallet wood can be hit-and-miss. Some of it is just so lousy that it's not really worth the time to gently bust it apart into useable planks. On the other hand, some pallets are made with woods that may be common in

Tiny Words of
Wisdom

## ON SHELVING

**Looking for a place to put a shelf? Think between the wall studs. Typical wall framing allows for a 14½-inch shelf between the studs. Just make sure you only try this on interior walls. Doing this on exterior walls would compromise your insulation.**

— **GEOFF BAKER,**
*founder and owner of*
*Westcoast Outbuildings*
*(Vancouver)*

**When thinking about maximizing space, look up! The average homeowner only uses about five feet of their available eight or more. Consider adding shelves up high on the wall. They can hold items that you rarely use and can be accessed by a step stool when needed.**

— **ANDREW ODOM,**
*tiny-house dweller,*
*podcast host, and blogger at*
*TinyRevolution.us*

a place like Brazil but are considered exotic and interesting to people like you and me. And shipping pallets, also known as forklift pallets, often are made of oak. Usually you can tell an oak pallet from pine (or other softwood) right off the bat when you try to lift it; oak is much heavier. It's also expensive, so the effort of reclaiming oak from pallets can be very worthwhile.

Pallets are free at many locales, such as behind industrial park businesses, hardware stores, and any retailers of bulky, heavy items (woodstove shops, for instance). Often all you have to do is ask. You'll need a truck or trailer to haul off more than one or two, though. Then there's the disassembly. Some folks use *pallet busters* — long, crowbar-like tools with forked ends — to speed up the process. And you can find plenty of online tutorials (on YouTube and the like) showing several ways to get it done.

The most important thing to look out for is the grading or identifying stamp on a pallet. The pallets you want to **use** are stamped with a big old "HT," indicating that the wood was heat-treated to kill any possibly invasive insects before it made its journey. The pallets you want to **avoid** carry an "MB" or "MT" stamp. This stands for methyl bromide, a fungicide; you wouldn't want to spray this on your toast, so don't use the wood for your new home. Regardless, even with clean-looking "HT" pallets, it's never a bad idea to brush, then spray them down before use, as who knows what used to sit atop them?

There are a ton of things you can use pallet wood for. There are more than a few books on the subject, as well as dedicated websites and instructional videos. Among the most common uses are flooring and wall cladding. While time-consuming, this gives any home a great, multicolored look — all with rustic, natural woods. I've also made quite a few Adirondack chairs and benches out of the stuff, as well as bookshelves, toolboxes, and garden planters. I've even used the thicker struts (often 2x4s or 2x3s) for actual framing, and I've gone so far as using whole pallets as mini "budget decks" or landings on my backwoods cabins.

## Lumber

Don't forget that lingering out there in garages, sheds, and workshops 'round the world is a veritable treasure trove of nearly or completely free lumber that

once was purchased by overzealous do-it-yourselfers who never realized their dreams of building a seven-level tree house, ark, or homemade time machine. This is why it's important to be outgoing and vocal about your future projects, interests, and needs. By making it known that I'm always on the prowl for materials, I've had many people offer up unused lumber piles to me for nothing, on trade, or for a ridiculously small amount of cash. Craigslist is another place where homeowners and carpenters often offer up their overstock. Best of all, though, is the free garage-clean-out lumber I've found street-side. I won't say that I stumble upon this situation all the time, but it isn't as elusive as a Bigfoot sighting,

flock of dodo birds, or albino rhino, either. Keep those eyes peeled.

However you come by it, salvaged lumber can give a build a custom look in addition to saving you loot. If you're aiming for a distressed look or a certain patina, there's no better way to achieve this than with wood that already has that genuine aura about it. And this is much easier than trying to reproduce the look of antique wood with new stock, expensive tools, too much time, and chemicals! If rough and vintage wood isn't your thing, keep in mind that not all free wood is going to be paint-laden and worn. With a little looking, and word of mouth, you'll probably find just what you need.

As a final tip, plan ahead and start to harbor materials early. A shed will do wonders to keep your materials safe and dry until they're needed, but on the low end of the spectrum, even just storing them under a six-dollar tarp will be sufficient — at least for a bit. Add in a good dose of patience and persistence while hunting for all this stuff and, again, you'll be just fine.

**Tiny Words of Wisdom ON CREATIVE CONVENIENCE**

Install hooks under your kitchen cabinets for storing pots, pans, coffee cups, and any other things you use frequently. This keeps them easily accessible and out of the cabinets themselves. Hooks are also beneficial (and very affordable) on your closet walls and doors so you can vertically store bags, dog leashes, hats, cleaning supplies, and just about anything you can think of.

— **ALEX PINO,** *blogger at TinyHouseTalk.com, Tiny House Newsletter*

# HERE'S WHERE I LIKE TO LOOK

You don't have to be the luckiest lad or lass alive to come across good, useful, and nearly free materials. You don't even have to be that bright or hardworking. Better yet, finding the future bones of your home or retreat can be fun. Since you never know what you're going to stumble across, it's almost like a treasure hunt. To make things easier for you, I've compiled a list of locales and avenues I've found to be fruitful in my years and years of architectural "picking." I must warn you, though: even the most highly reviewed Salvageaholics Anonymous groups often fail to break the habit, once formed.

## Tiny Words of Wisdom ON SECRET COMPARTMENTS

No matter how well you plan out your storage, you might still be left with a "dead space" that you can't make much functional use of. Typical offenders are spaces stuck between, under, behind, or on top of cabinets, drawers, or other built-in furniture. One way to put every inch to work is to install some James Bond secret compartments! While you might not be able to keep much inside your weird triangle space between your loft joist and your built-in closet, it will delight friends when you pop it open to get your extra batteries or personal documents . . . top-secret documents, of course! One pro tip is to use magnets or baby-proof cabinet latches to secure your secret door.

— **JOE COOVER**, *tiny-house dweller, blogger at LongStoryShortHouse.com*

- Yard sales (aka tag sales, garage sales)
- Estate sales (farms especially)
- Flea markets
- Thrift shops

- Craigslist.com
- Freecycle.org
- Construction sites (with permission)
- Habitat for Humanity ReStores (and similar retailers)

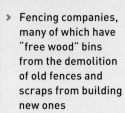

Town dumps . . . ahem, "transfer stations"

Private junkyards/ scrap metal yards (for car seating, metal parts, woodstoves, and more)

- Fencing companies, many of which have "free wood" bins from the demolition of old fences and scraps from building new ones
- Curbs during trash day (I call it "suburban curbin'")
- Boatyards (lots of wood gets tossed at these places, not to mention other materials, tarps, and interesting hardware)

- Recycling centers or "take it or leave it" stations at dumps
- College towns right around graduation or move-in time (for furniture and decor)
- Freebie piles behind chain hardware stores (most stores will let you have some of their "junk lumber" if you ask)
- Dumpsters, for the more daring (Who cares?! Go for it!)

## Dear Neighbor

Since I don't mind spreading the good word if it means keeping more things out of landfills, I will tell you that one of my best tactics, with a success rate over 50 percent, is to drop mailbox notes. No, not love letters, but rather "I love that crud of yours" letters. Seriously. If I happen to see huge fallen limbs as potential firewood, a downed line of fencing being heaped for removal, or a seemingly long-forgotten pile of metal roofing or tongue-and-groove siding, I grab a pen and pad I keep in my van and scrawl a little note that reads something like this:

*Hey, I noticed you had a pile of _____ in your back-yard, and I'm working on a DIY project right now — on a very, very tight budget. If you're ever looking to get rid of the stuff, I'll haul it away for you and save you the hassle, or maybe even give you a few bucks for it [or case of beer, help with yard work . . .]. If interested, let me know. I'd really appreciate it, as my funds are limited and I could certainly put that stuff to very good use.*

*[Name and phone number]*

You might also add: "When I'm done with my project I'll be sure to send you a photo of it, if you'd like!"

Of course, you'll have to tailor the letter to the situation. You might not even want to suggest money because if they're willing to get rid of their goods for nothing you've now shown your hand and put money in their minds. Use your own judgment, but always be sure to be polite and keep it short, sweet, and legible. This little method has worked for me many, many times and once yielded a nearly suspension-killing trailerload of 8-foot-long, true 1x8 planks. I'm smiling right now as I think about that find and how many projects that score has since gone into. People often tear down decks and pay someone for the demo work, so there's another avenue you might want to stroll down— money *and* material, all from "junk."

Another overlooked means to acquisition is to simply make it known that you'll soon be undertaking a project and are looking for secondhand materials. "If your neighbors know, the junk will flow" is a goofy little saying I often share with students. You'll be shocked to see how much useful material will be saved and offered to you — sometimes *too* much of it, so be warned.

# THE BUDGET-AND-SALVAGE CHEAT SHEET

> Subflooring is the flooring (until you tire of it, or it gets beaten)

> Concrete slabs work as flooring.

> Build on skids (two or more 4x4 or larger wood timbers) — it's cheap and quick and makes it easier to move the building.

> Set structural posts in packed, crushed stone or on stone instead of time-consuming concrete.

> Solid-wood interior doors, when coated and protected, can be used as exterior doors, if security isn't as much of a concern.

> Car siding (single-layered, tongue-and-groove wood siding), or even well-painted plywood exterior siding, works well and looks good on seasonal cabins or retreats.

> Look for "HT" (heat-treated) pallet wood to use for shelving, wall coverage, and even floors.

> Smooth, poly-coated scrap flooring is heavy but can be used to cover a wall and even works like a dry-erase board.

> Ugly recycled lumber and studs can be hidden within walls, as long as they're sturdy and sound.

> Make your own trim from furring strips with a table saw or router.

> Don't be afraid to let the materials dictate the design/build.

> Good, free windows are everywhere . . . or you can make your own from stereo glass, clear container tops, etc.

> Look for free paint at recycling depots; and don't forget to make your own paint colors — take those freebie paints and get creative.

> Save or collect scrap wood for things like bracing, blocking, shelving, or shims.

> Even the lousiest hollow-core doors often have decent hinges and hardware.

> Make your own "hardware" accessories — curved-branch drawer pulls, bent/drilled silverware for handles, rake-head wine glass holders . . .

> If you don't need sonic privacy, consider curtains for doors.

> Be on the lookout for junk shelving that doesn't look too junky. Try streetside dresser drawers, cleaned, painted, and mounted against the wall.

> You can use non-pressure-treated wood for a base, but paint the wood with freebie paints (two or three coats) to protect it. It's not ideal, but it'll do.

> Pool liner roofing? It works.

> Don't be afraid to reach for the unusual: a car hood could become a front door overhang, for instance, or a heat shield for a woodstove.

Found wood
with freebie
paints

# decor on a dime

**8**

**A CABIN, SHELTER, OR TINY HOME** can feel like a cold, hollow shell without some comfortable and well-thought-out decor. It would only be cheating yourself to peter out, toss in the towel, and shortcut things once you're so close to completing your mini-haven. I also understand that if a decent amount of money and time has been gobbled up by your new project, the last thing you'll be gung-ho about is blowing a chunk of change on items to outfit your cabin. But I have a few tricks up my sleeve that seem to work well in a financial pinch. These are not one-size-fits-all solutions, but they have worked well for me in the past and might help you, too. Who doesn't want to save money when decorating?

# PLB

"PLB" is a term that I started using behind the scenes while doing a good deal of hosting and design work for my YouTube show, then later HGTV and the DIY Network. It began to stick as a catchphrase when we had completed a build and the episode's remaining funds were low. "Hit it with the PLB!" became the joke — but it worked *every* time and always made for a cozy, funky, inviting, and uniquely designed space.

So what the heck am I talking about? What exactly does PLB mean? Platypus Liberation Boycott? Particularly Lazy Bison? Nope. It's the lowest common denominator of decor, the three affordable things I find myself turning to: pillows, lanterns, and books. It sounds crazy, I

know, but aside from the essentials you might already have — a bed, a chair, etc. — there are few quicker ways to warm up a space. Comfort (pillows), light (lanterns), and intelligence, intrigue, and eclecticism (books) are all brought forth with this little trick.

## Pillows

To delve a little deeper (not that I want to hold forth on pillow selection here), let's start with the P. Pillows come in 5,009.3 varieties, shapes, and colors and can be had, or made, inexpensively. Heck, I've even grabbed a few pillows and cushions off of trashday couches before. Egads! Gasp! Calm down. A little time on high heat in the dryer and all germs and threats are usually nullified. Washing pillows in an industrial machine might be a good idea too. As for stains, you're on your own, so I suggest you employ some selective picking to avoid them.

But back to the point: the P is a means to an inviting end. Pictures and paintings are great, but can you sit on,

---

**Tiny Words of Wisdom ON DECOR**

In a tiny house, there's not much space for knickknacks or things that don't have a specific purpose. They just add clutter. We have a few paintings and meaningful pieces of artwork in our house, but for the most part we decorated with things that are useful. We kept our kitchen open instead of hiding utensils, pots, and pans in cabinets. Our glasses, mugs, and plates were all handmade by friends or picked out from thrift stores. We love how funky and mismatched they are, and displaying that out on open shelves is part of what gives the room its character. We also tore down some of the paneling in the kitchen and built a spice shelf into the backside of the exposed wall. We keep grains and beans in glass jars on high shelves and hang our pots from hooks on the wall. In the living space, books and folded blankets are like paintings and fill the room with texture and color.

— **CHRISTOPHER SMITH AND MERETE MUELLER,**
*producers of the film* Tiny: A Story about Living Small

sleep with, snuggle against, and prop up your head with a cheap Norman Rockwell reproduction? Not likely, and definitely not without getting a kink in your neck. Also, keep in mind that once you tire of a certain pillow's style, instead of chucking it you can simply slip a new cover over it, bringing some new vibrancy into your home or hut. IKEA has a great selection of pillowcases, and in some wild patterns, too. An obnoxiously pink pillowcase with a modern-art owl on it? Yup, they got it (and I bought it!).

## Lanterns

Moving along to the L. Lanterns work in much the same way as pillows: they subtly convey a sense of simplicity, they can be very inexpensive, they give your cabin or hideout a certain glow and ambiance, and they're versatile in their look. Depending on its style, a lantern can create almost any feel, from rustic or quaint to wild, modern, and daring. In my arsenal of archaic lights, which I've amassed over the years, you'll find ceramic owls, glass orbs, clay classics, vintage Dietz railroad

cans, tikilike lights, and even angular modern versions of candle lamps. I might also mention that yard sales seem to be brimming with these things, so acquiring a nice one or two can be quite wallet-friendly. Oil lamps are great too, and some are absolute works of art. Oil lamps give out a lot of heat in addition to light, and standard electric lamps with incandescent bulbs deliver some heat too, perhaps even enough to keep a tiny space comfortable. **Note:** You must have adequate ventilation and a carbon monoxide detector in a microstructure if you burn oil lamps or candles inside.

## Books

Lastly, there's the B. "Deek, I mean, c'mon, who doesn't have too many of these things already? It's the era of downloadable books, man! And you're asking us to harbor even *more* printed matter?" Relax, relax . . .

Books are another item you might already have plenty of, and you're bound to find them at yard sales, flea markets, thrift shops, and, naturally, at new and used bookstores. I've

# LANTERN NIGHT-LIGHTS

In my off-grid cabin up in Vermont, I've started a cool little tradition that ties in with my continually growing collection of lanterns. Each night when the kids go to bed, they get to select one oil lamp or candle lantern to leave burning as a night-light (until we parents go to sleep). One night they might choose to fall asleep to the warm glow of a red-glass lantern, while the next it may be one that bathes the cabin in a blue hue. They take turns each night on who gets to pick. Of course, if they don't behave Daddy gets to pick his favorite: the dartlike, amber-sided Moroccan lantern — always. Just recently I nabbed a metal lantern shaped like a tiny house, believe it or not, so we might have a new contender for the top spot.

found some great ones in the sale pile at my town library for 25 cents. I like to think of it this way: these tomes, whether on shelves or laid out coffee-table style, are "useable art." Comic books are very much the same. Yeah, a good painting or picture is worth a thousand words, as they say, but a book, well, it can be appealing to look it, but it can also be grabbed up to offer thousands and thousands of words. Furthermore, in a pinch you

## Tiny Words of Wisdom ON DECOR

I love the idea of taking vintage picture frames, mounting them to walls, and hanging necklaces and such within the frame on little hooks. You're outwardly displaying beautiful jewelry as art instead of hiding it away in a box where it's apt to become tangled. In general, try to store artlike objects in the open. Why shove a nice guitar under a bed, eating up that storage space that could be used for other items, when it could be cradled up on a wall?

— **AUSTIN HAY,** *tiny-house owner/builder*

can use a book to stabilize the leg of a wobbly table, swat a pesky fly, throw at a burglar, weigh down paperwork, or, if the book is especially lousy, create heat in the form of kindling. I hear that Snooki's biography carries a lot of BTUs . . .

I'm a real sucker for old scouting books as well as how-to guides. My rule of thumb: I'll rarely pay over two dollars for a book, and it has to be something I'd actually be interested in reading or is just so off-the-wall that it's bound to be a conversation starter, or at least a comical display piece. Extremely dated titles, like *How to Cure Gout with Leeches, and Other Such Remedies*, and *Cinderblocks: The Poor Man's Facelift* also provide entertainment and some kitsch.

# MORE TO GUSSY UP YOUR SPACE

It's time to stuff a few measly dollars in your pants pocket and have a blast budget-shopping for your little abode's future decor! You might surprise yourself with how good you can make it look, and for almost nothing. What have you got to lose? Here are some more ideas to get you started.

**OLD GLASS BOTTLES** are ever-present at junk shops and tag sales. I have some great ones that are loaded with

you can't really lose. And if you ever tire of, or accidentally break, your little gems of decor, they're fit for recycling.

**MIRRORS** run the gamut in looks and style and can make any space feel bigger when used effectively. I'm sure you've walked into a bar and initially thought it was twice as big as it really was. That's the space-trickery of mirrors.

**EXTRA BLANKETS** are always handy, and it's nice to have a few interesting and colorful ones kicking around for cold nights or for a guest to use.

**OLD PAINTINGS** can warm up a room and add some vibrancy, and they're great conversation starters. Back when I lived in Boston, my roommates and I had a ridiculously bad oil painting of a turkey-necked, aristocratic-looking old man smoking a pipe. Who was this guy? What possessed the artist to attempt to capture the likeness of this strange and seemingly random person? Guests would always comment on it. My current home has a still-life painting of a bug-eyed Boston terrier, which gets the same reaction. I found this particular piece at an antiques mall in central Maine. Flipping yard-sale paintings can be profitable too (funds for your cabin?).

character: a horse-head-shaped liquor bottle, a cobalt-blue paint thinner container, cracked-style glass vases, a green glass truck that once held Avon cologne, a vintage Wild West–looking whiskey bottle, and more. They can hold flowers, foods, liquids, and other assorted items, all while being very interesting to look at — especially if placed where light can pass through them. Budget-wise,

**VINTAGE TOYS.** Even if you're the serious, far-too-grown-up type who wouldn't be caught dead displaying some sort of childish, trivial item (in which case you really need to lighten up!), at least consider that toys are art. A lot of planning, design consideration, and time goes into crafting toys. As with yard-sale paintings, my stance is "the more bizarre, the better." I visited a great tree-house-style apartment in Brooklyn a while back, and I can still picture the little wooden toy robot standing on a bookshelf. This unique piece added color and interest to an otherwise plain old shelf full of books. It sent the message that these people aren't afraid to have fun. I later found that these robots were made in Brooklyn by a company called Areaware, and naturally I grabbed one up.

**UNUSUAL CHAIRS** are yet another way to work functional artistic elements into a home. A shell-backed metal deck chair or unique armchair can become a focal point or be used to distract the eye from an undesirable or sparsely furnished portion of a room. Call it dual-purpose decorating.

**A FUNKY, HOMEMADE COFFEE TABLE OR SIDE TABLE** can be fun and functional. The examples that

roll off assembly lines and land in department stores usually are pretty boring. Instead, try thinking outside the box to create a visually unique piece with a story behind it. "See that li'l coffee table over yonder? Well, that was made out of

an old cable spool, with some roadside wood and some pipe fittings and flanges slapped on for legs." When I eventually get tired of my recycled-furniture builds, I sell them and begin work on their replacements. Sawed-off tables (with shortened legs) can work as low consoles as well. In my Rock Shed (page 69) I have a rather obnoxiously orange one that I love.

Tiny Words of Wisdom
## ON DUAL FUNCTION-ALITY

Under the stairs is a great place for cubby storage, whether accessed via drawers in the steps or just as open shelving, and steps themselves can give you a good amount of storage for bulky items like blankets and shoes.

— **MACY MILLER,**
*tiny-house owner/builder,*
*blogger at minimotives.com*

**WOODEN CRATES.** I've found many vintage crates for free or very little. They're great to use for makeshift seats, ottomans, or record and book storage and can even be secured to a wall as shelving. Keep them rustic on the outside and give them a single coat of paint on the inside, and you'll have some truly fun and attractive wall shelves.

**RUGS.** Don't be afraid to "rug it up." I love hardwood floors, but they can make a space look and feel cold. Rugs are easily replaceable when they wear out or when you just get tired of them. There are some very unusual ones out there too, should you choose to express your inner weirdo. If you like the rustic look, braided rugs seem to last the longest, especially good ones. Remember that in a small space a rug receives regular heavy traffic, so pick a winner.

**A HAMMOCK.** There's nothing quite like it. Hammocks are affordable, lightweight, and dang comfortable. Aside from being quickly assembled sleep spots, hammocks can be hung as storage cradles or, in narrower spaces (with ends closer together), as sling seats. When they're not in use you can leave them half-hung (adding a little pizzazz to a corner), or you can wad 'em up and stuff 'em into just about any tiny storage nook, or even a pillowcase.

**PLANTS,** live or fake. Including flora in your little domicile will add a natural, organic touch to the setting and, depending on your selection, might give people the illusion that you have a green thumb! It'll be our little secret. Live plants can even cleanse the air in small spaces. An array of unusual, recycled homemade pots and containers might be nice too.

**HOMEMADE ART** is another budget decor item that can either go incredibly well or horribly wrong, depending on your artistic abilities or, well, lack thereof. The point here is that you're adding a one-of-a-kind touch to your home that can serve as a conversation piece and cost close to nothing. You might even try making some swinging wood-backed art that doubles as interior shutters.

**FUNKY WINDOW TRIM OR COLORFUL CURTAINS.** There's no rule saying that interior window trim needs to be colorless, bland, and rigid. So why not live it up a little? Natural trim works fine, but add in some color and you'll be pleasantly surprised with the results. If you're not into painting, try going for salvaged wood with a little wear or weathering. New, virgin wood contrasted with vintage, stained, or time-grayed planks looks fantastic — the "coloring" has already been done for you. You're decorating and enhancing a room by doing practically nothing.

**DARE TO DRAW ON YOUR WALLS.**
Why not? This could be the cheapest wall art of all. It's daring and unconventional, but any half-skilled artist with a giant Sharpie marker can go to town on a blank wall with interesting results. If you later tire of the work, or you mess up, just paint over it.

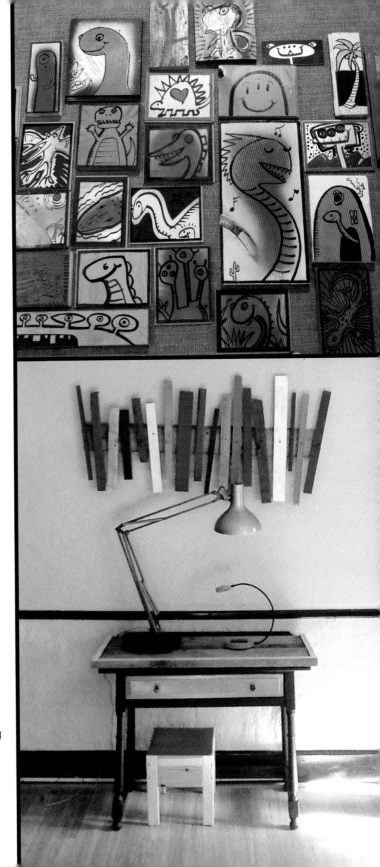

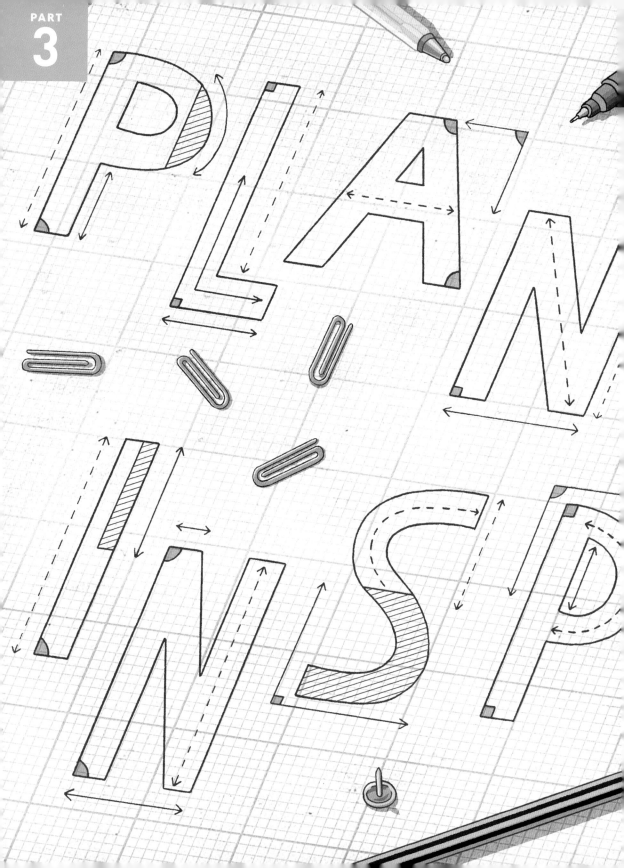

# six
# from the
# masters

## 9

**WITHIN THIS SMALL BUT HAND-SELECTED GROUP OF PLANS,** you'll find possibilities for backyard offices, sheds, playhouses, tree houses, hobby shacks, vacation cabins, and possibly even tiny houses. Some are seasonal units but could easily be insulated and improved to extend their use, depending on your climate. All of them are small, of course. The plans are here to give you ideas and to serve as basic construction guidelines. Feel free to enlarge, shrink, tweak, and craft them to your needs. Each offering includes a Construction Basics section providing a quick overview of the build to supplement the plan drawings. This assumes some familiarity with standard construction technique, so if you're a newbie, it's a good idea to sit down with an expert to get a sense of what the project might involve.

# THE SAWTOOTH

**96 square feet**

**Will Yount,
Hummingbird
Tiny Spaces**

**A** JACK OF MANY TRADES, and a carpenter and small-space designer by profession, Will Yount, of the design company Hummingbird Tiny Spaces, has been at it for decades now, crafting one-of-a-kind, affordable cabins, backyard retreats, and full-out homes, both small and large, in the greater Tennessee area. He's based out of the music epicenter that is Nashville, so it's no surprise that most of his clientele are musicians looking for backyard recording studios and rehearsal cabins. Regardless of use, Will's work offers great flexibility, simple construction, affordability, and even portability, if need be. The Sawtooth is no exception. What I love most is its departure from the gable roofline, which seems to dominate most small builds.

**Will offers this handful of building tips to keep in mind as you work:**

> Measure twice, cut once. Always double-check level and square.

> The foundation is important. Everything sits on it.

> It always seems to take longer than you think it will, but all you can do in a day is all you can do. Tomorrow's another day.

> Some jobs are harder than they look. It's easy to underestimate cost or what or how much you can do.

> Make sure you check building codes and property lines. You don't want to have to move your building.

> Think about the future. Build a good roof and shell that won't leak.

> Pay attention to detail. A quarter of an inch might not seem like a big deal, but they all add up.

> Be safe!

## CONSTRUCTION BASICS

The Sawtooth's design is lean and straightforward, with conventionally framed walls, basic shed-style roofs, and a simple custom wall for the clerestory windows. The three large walls add versatility to the interior space and make it easy to modify size and placement of doors and windows.

**Main Floor**

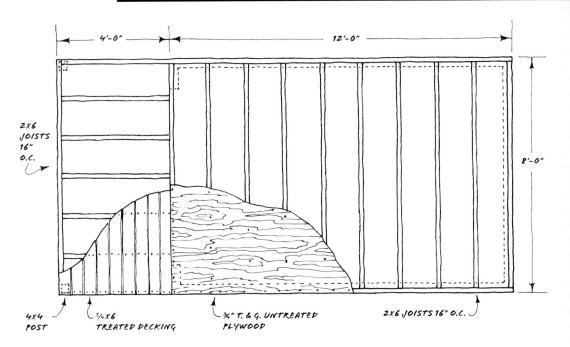

2X6 JOISTS 16" O.C.

4'-0"    12'-0"

8'-0"

4X4 POST    ⁵/₄X6 TREATED DECKING    ¾" T. & G. UNTREATED PLYWOOD    2X6 JOISTS 16" O.C.

## FOUNDATION

The foundation type can be based on the building site and local code requirements, as applicable. Standard options may include full-length timber skids or a series of concrete blocks placed at regular intervals. The foundation should provide even support under the cabin floor and deck areas and prevent ground contact with the floor frame.

## FLOOR

The floor frame consists of two sections, so you don't need lumber longer than 12 feet. Sheathe the cabin floor with standard (non-treated) ¾-inch tongue-and-groove plywood. Deck the porch floor with treated ⁵/₄x6 decking boards.

## WALLS

The cabin walls are conventionally framed with 2x4s at 16 inches on center. On the front wall, the door header and the beam below the upper windows are built with 2x4s sandwiched over ½-inch plywood. The porch roof is supported at the front by treated 4x4 posts. Sheathing can be ½-inch OSB or plywood, and you can use any standard siding material, or use plywood siding to serve as both sheathing and siding.

**Side Wall**

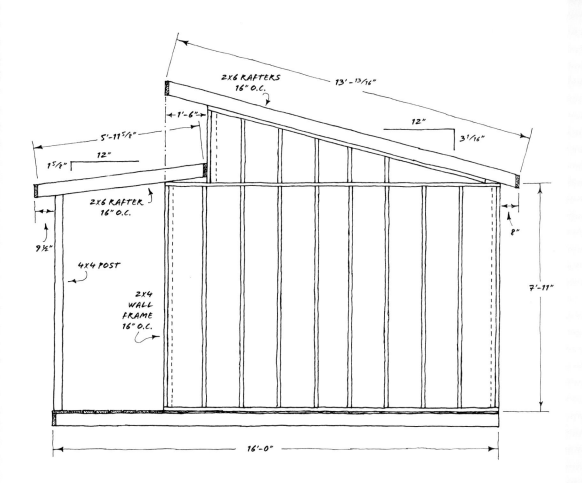

2X6 RAFTERS 16" O.C.

13'-13/16"

1'-6"

12"

3 1/16"

5'-11 5/8"

12"

1 5/8"

2X6 RAFTER 16" O.C.

8"

9½"

4X4 POST

2X4 WALL FRAME 16" O.C.

7'-11"

16'-0"

## Rear Wall

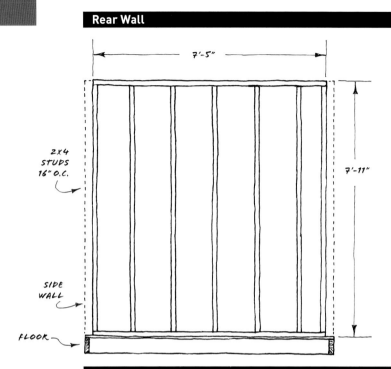

7'-5"

2X4 STUDS 16" O.C.

7'-11"

SIDE WALL

FLOOR

## Main Front Wall

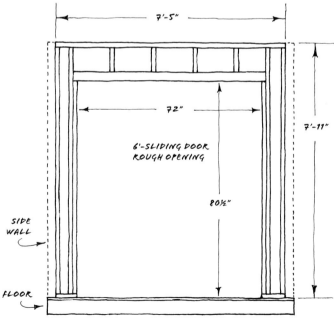

7'-5"

72"

6'-SLIDING DOOR ROUGH OPENING

80½"

7'-11"

SIDE WALL

FLOOR

*ELEVATION*

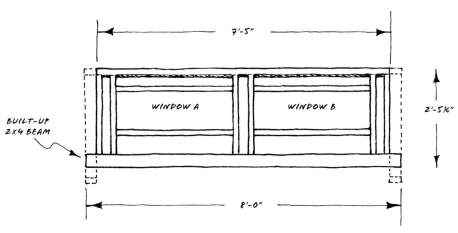

7'-5"

WINDOW A          WINDOW B

2'-5½"

BUILT-UP
2X4 BEAM

8'-0"

*BEAM DETAIL*

WINDOW ROUGH
OPENINGS A & B:
2'-11" WIDE
BY 11 ½" HIGH

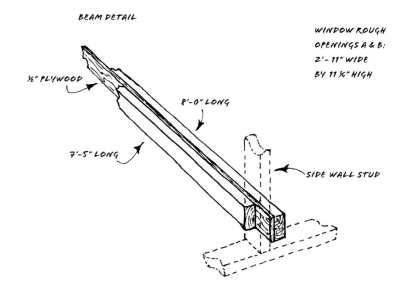

½" PLYWOOD

8'-0" LONG

7'-5" LONG

SIDE WALL STUD

## LOFT

Build the optional loft platform with 2x4s and plywood, anchoring into the side- and rear-wall studs. The platform shown is 5 x 8 feet, but its size can be modified as desired.

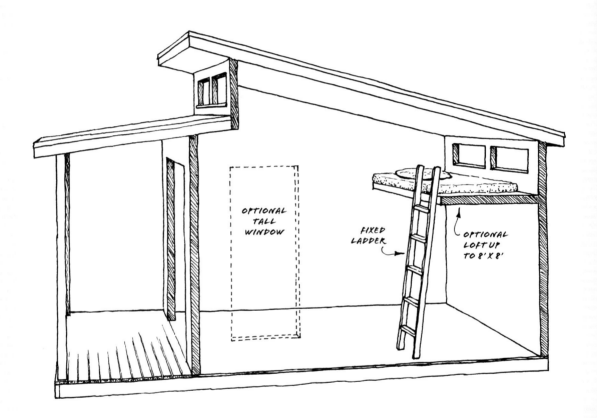

## WINDOWS AND DOORS

The cabin door frame is sized at 72 x 80½ inches for a standard-size slider or hinged patio doors. Sizes and locations of the door and all windows can be modified to fit salvaged, prefab, or homemade units and custom layouts. Adding windows to the rear wall — such as above the loft, if included — increases light and ventilation in the cabin.

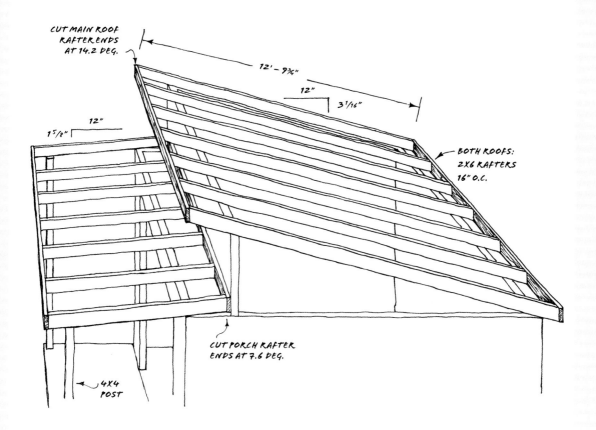

CUT MAIN ROOF RAFTER ENDS AT 14.2 DEG.

12' - 9¾"

12"

3¹/₁₆"

12"

1⁵/₈"

BOTH ROOFS: 2X6 RAFTERS 16" O.C.

CUT PORCH RAFTER ENDS AT 7.6 DEG.

4X4 POST

## ROOF

The rafters are 2x6 but can be 2x4 if appropriate for local conditions. At the other end of the spectrum, some framing modifications might be needed for snowy climates, such as adding a full-length wall stud directly under the short outer studs on the upper wall. Sheathe the roof with ½-inch OSB or plywood. Most standard roofing materials are suitable, but roof slope is a consideration. Metal roofing looks good on shed-style roofs, and most types are suitable for the 3¹/₁₆-in-12 slope on the cabin roof. Check with manufacturers' specifications for roofing over the 1⁵/₈-in-12 slope of the porch roof.

# THE MICRO DOGTROT CABIN

**102 square feet**

**Holly Gomez, A Place Imagined**

**H**OLLY GOMEZ, a mom with a background in architecture, has always had a passion for designing tiny spaces that encourage self-expression and open-ended play. As a child she spent summers building forts and play spaces in the woods near her house. She would sketch out plans, then rush outside to play. It only made sense that as an adult, she would design grown-up buildings. Holly graduated in 2003 with a bachelor's degree in architecture from Mississippi State University and gained experience designing larger-scale buildings.

In 2009 Holly started the blog *A Place Imagined* as a way of documenting her research on playhouses. The blog, full of endless inspiration and helpful tips, is now a resource for anyone considering building a play space of their own. In 2011 Holly left her corporate job and officially founded the company A Place Imagined, where she now designs play spaces full-time. Playhouse plans, as well as fully assembled playhouses, can be purchased through her website.

The Micro Dogtrot Cabin features great use of both indoor and outdoor living space. The partially enclosed area opposite the cabin houses a bench or can be outfitted with an outdoor kitchen and/or storage units. Like the other offerings in this book, it is simple, sturdy, and affordable. It could also be altered in many ways, as shown on page 221. Additionally, the cabin could be widened to 8 feet to take full advantage of stock-length lumber and to make the interior, and especially the little loft, slightly roomier. One could also increase the height and pitch of the roof for even more sleep loft space.

## CONSTRUCTION BASICS

The Micro Dogtrot Cabin is 7 feet x 14 feet 8 inches and stands at 11 feet 6 inches
tall. That footprint makes it slightly over 102 square feet. Check with your
local building department about requirements for small structures. Some towns
require a permit for anything over 100 square feet.

**Floor Plan**

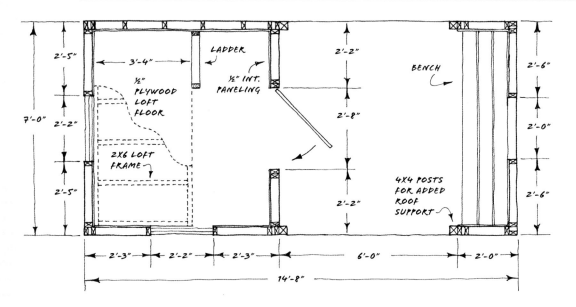

## FOUNDATION

The foundation can be as simple as six (or more) concrete blocks partially buried atop a 4-inch or thicker layer of compacted gravel. The tops of the blocks should extend at least 2 inches above grade.

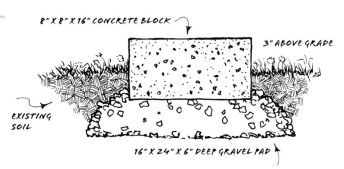

8" X 8" X 16" CONCRETE BLOCK

3" ABOVE GRADE

EXISTING SOIL

16" X 24" X 6" DEEP GRAVEL PAD

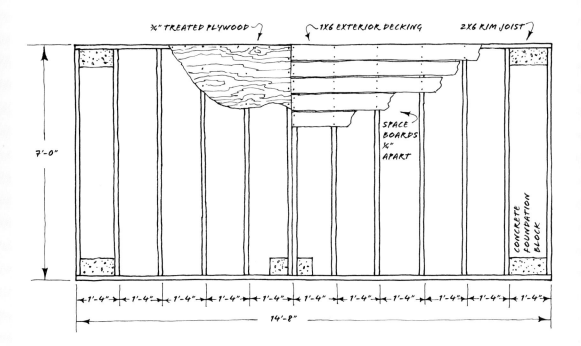

¾" TREATED PLYWOOD

1X6 EXTERIOR DECKING

2X6 RIM JOIST

SPACE BOARDS ¼" APART

CONCRETE FOUNDATION BLOCK

7'-0"

1'-4" 1'-4" 1'-4" 1'-4" 1'-4" 1'-4" 1'-4" 1'-4" 1'-4" 1'-4" 1'-4"

14'-8"

## FLOOR

The floor is framed with pressure-treated 2x6 joists and gets a double joist at the door-wall for the enclosed cabin space. This is where the floor deck transitions from ¾-inch treated plywood sheathing (for the interior floor) to treated 1x6 decking for the exterior floor. Gap the decking boards for drainage.

## Side Wall with Window

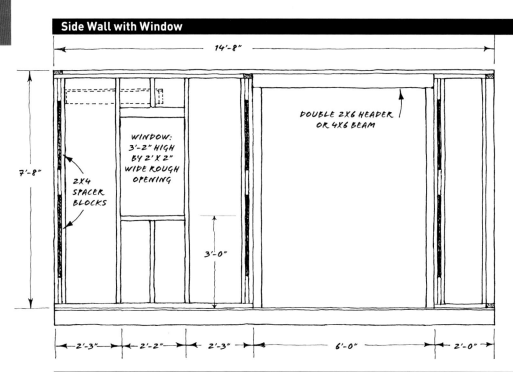

14'-8"

7'-8"

DOUBLE 2X6 HEADER
OR 4X6 BEAM

WINDOW:
3'-2" HIGH
BY 2' X 2"
WIDE ROUGH
OPENING

2X4
SPACER
BLOCKS

3'-0"

2'-3"    2'-2"    2'-3"    6'-0"    2'-0"

## Cabin Door Wall

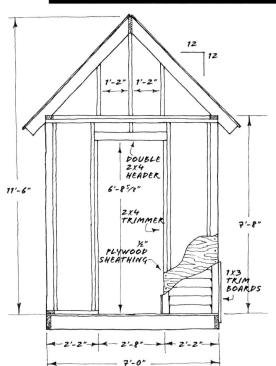

12
12

1'-2"  1'-2"

11'-6"

DOUBLE
2X4
HEADER

6'-8⅝"

2X4
TRIMMER

½"
PLYWOOD
SHEATHING

1X3
TRIM
BOARDS

7'-8"

2'-2"    2'-8"    2'-2"

7'-0"

## WALLS

The cabin and covered bench/ storage area have conventionally framed 2x4 walls. You can modify the window and door openings as needed to fit any prefab, salvaged, or homemade units. Only one of the cabin side walls gets a window, but you could quite easily add more.

## Cabin End Wall

Frame, raise, and brace the cabin walls first, then add the 4x4 posts at the corners of the porch opening. Span across the porch with two double 2x6 beams. The 2x4 double top plate over the long side walls covers the cabin wall, porch beam, and right end wall, tying all three together.

Sheathe the walls with ½-inch OSB or plywood sheathing, followed by trim and any desired siding materials. Alternatively, you can use plywood siding as both sheathing and siding.

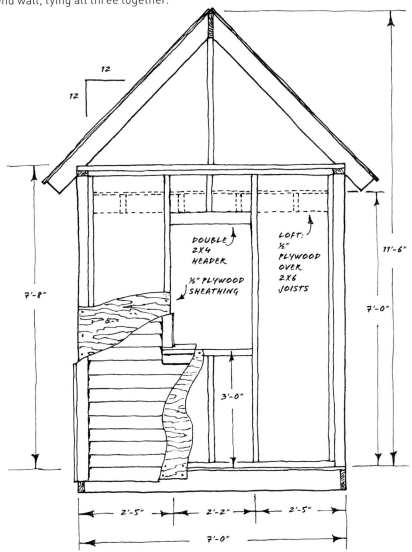

12

12

DOUBLE
2X4
HEADER

½" PLYWOOD
SHEATHING

LOFT:
½"
PLYWOOD
OVER
2X6
JOISTS

7'-8"

5"

3'-0"

11'-6"

7'-0"

2'-5"     2'-2"     2'-5"

7'-0"

**Porch End Wall**

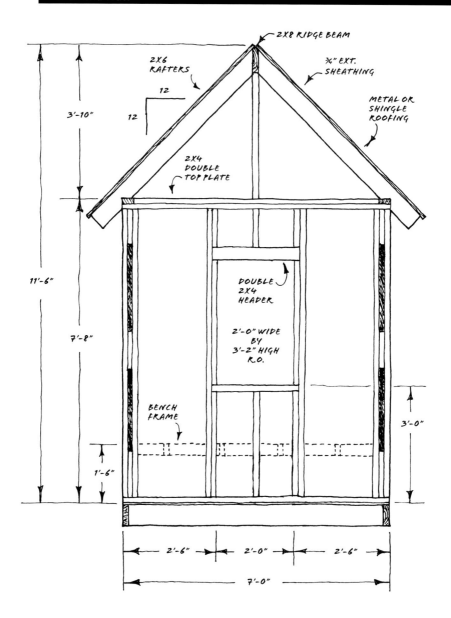

2X8 RIDGE BEAM

2X6 RAFTERS

12
12

¾" EXT. SHEATHING

METAL OR SHINGLE ROOFING

2X4 DOUBLE TOP PLATE

3'-10"

11'-6"

7'-8"

DOUBLE 2X4 HEADER

2'-0" WIDE BY 3'-2" HIGH R.O.

BENCH FRAME

3'-0"

1'-6"

2'-6"    2'-0"    2'-6"

7'-0"

## LOFT

Frame the loft with 2x6s, spacing the joists 16 inches on center and anchoring the frame into the studs of the three surrounding walls. Top the frame with ½-inch plywood. Build a homemade ladder with 2x4s. You can secure the ladder to the loft frame, or leave it unsecured so you can hang it on the windowless side wall of the cabin when it's not in use.

# ROOF

The roof frame has a continuous 2x8 ridge beam. Three sets of 2x6 "A" rafters define the three gable ends; seven sets of 2x6 "B" rafters fill in between. A 2x4 post helps support the ridge at each gable end. Sheathe the roof with ¾-inch plywood, overhanging the gable-wall studs by 3 inches and the rafter tails by 1 inch. Any standard roofing material is suitable. If you use shingles, fasten them with ½-inch roofing nails so the nails won't protrude below the sheathing.

## Roof Frame

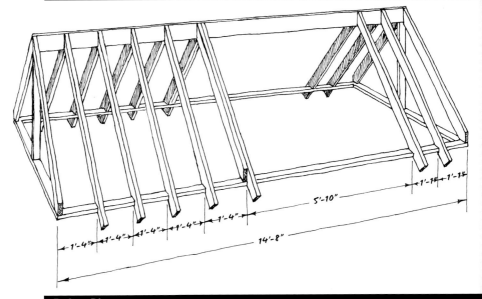

## Rafter Diagrams

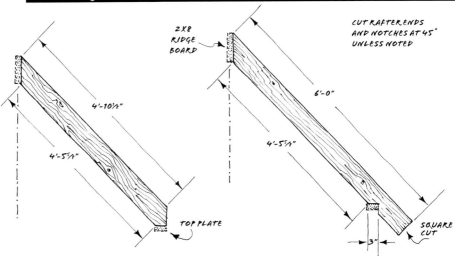

## DOOR AND WINDOWS

The basic plan calls for a prehung door and new or salvaged window units for three rectangular windows on the main walls. As an optional feature, the gabled space above the door gets four homemade triangular windows built with 2x2s. Ideally, the tall center windows are operable for ventilation. A set of salvaged windows also can work well here. Wrap the window rough opening with a single sill cut from a 2x8 and with 2x4s along the sloping sides.

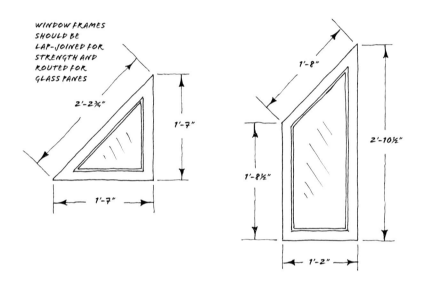

WINDOW FRAMES
SHOULD BE
LAP-JOINED FOR
STRENGTH AND
ROUTED FOR
GLASS PANES

2'-2¾"

1'-7"

1'-7"

1'-8"

2'-10½"

1'-8½"

1'-2"

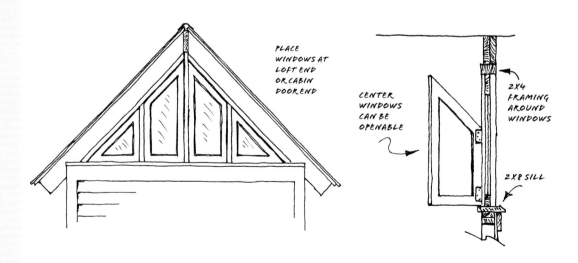

PLACE
WINDOWS AT
LOFT END
OR CABIN
DOOR END

CENTER
WINDOWS
CAN BE
OPENABLE

2X4
FRAMING
AROUND
WINDOWS

2X8 SILL

## Variation 1: Extended Roof with Screened-In Porch

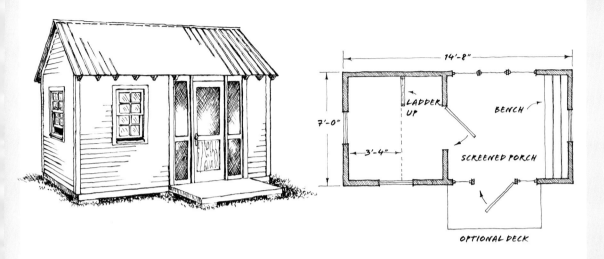

14'-8"

7'-0"

LADDER UP

BENCH

3'-4"

SCREENED PORCH

OPTIONAL DECK

## Variation 2: Extended Roof with Two Large Rooms

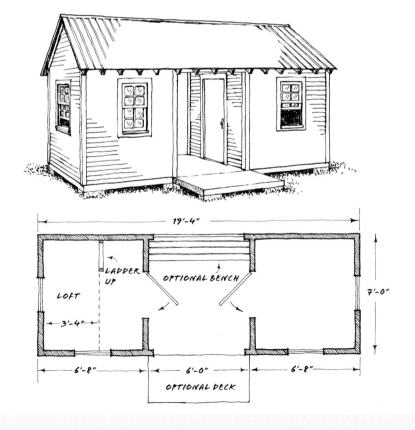

19'-4"

LADDER UP

OPTIONAL BENCH

LOFT

7'-0"

3'-4"

6'-8"

6'-0"

6'-8"

OPTIONAL DECK

# THE STILTED SLEEPER

**T**HE STILTED SLEEPER IS A COLLABORATION between me and a friend, Jay Shafer of Sebastopol, California's Four Lights Tiny Houses. Shafer is well known in the small-structure community, and he's often been credited as a key founder of the modern tiny-house movement — for good reason. Jay has lived in a tiny house, has built and designed tiny houses, currently lives in a very small home with his family of four, and has taught well over a hundred building and design workshops nationwide. He knows his stuff and lives, eats, sleeps, and breathes small structures. For this reason, and because our backgrounds and styles are so different, we thought it might be fun to team up on a design. "Let's just see what happens," we said.

**32 square feet, with additional outdoor living space beneath**

**Jay Shafer, Four Lights Tiny Houses, with Deek Diedricksen**

Jay, a pro in simplicity and efficiency, had been wanting to build a series of tiny, cubbylike sleeping sheds that could be dispersed on a property for guests and friends. These would require little money, effort, and time to build. I, having built many similar tiny single-sleepers or "escape pods" for reading or meditating or as offices, jumped in and thought, "I love it, but let's make it a tad more out-there and whimsical — yet still on a meager budget." The result is a stilted cabin with an underbelly area that can be used as a shelter for food preparation, sitting, staying out of the sun or rain, or even as a parking spot for a full-out picnic table. A hinged wall serves as a windbreak in the down position and transforms into an overhead patio shelter in the up position.

By lofting this simple gabled microhut, we've enhanced its window views, created a bit more privacy through its height, and added more security from woodland animals that might try to damage it. Access to the elevated cabin is provided by permanent stairs or a removable ladder, which you can take away to improve security when you're not a home. A built-in bench (facing a campfire, perhaps) could be added between the stilts.

## CONSTRUCTION BASICS

The cabin of the Stilted Sleeper has a lean frame of 2x2s built atop a floor deck made with a single 4 x 8-foot sheet of plywood. The stilts are 4x4 pressure-treated posts and have knee bracing for stability. As an option, you can anchor the structure for wind resistance by burying the posts (with or without concrete) below the frost line in your area.

**Framing Diagram**

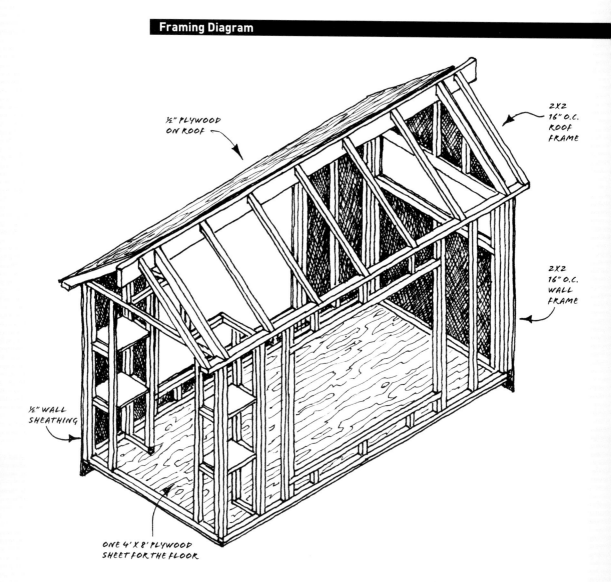

½" PLYWOOD
ON ROOF

2X2
16" O.C.
ROOF
FRAME

2X2
16" O.C.
WALL
FRAME

½" WALL
SHEATHING

ONE 4'X 8' PLYWOOD
SHEET FOR THE FLOOR

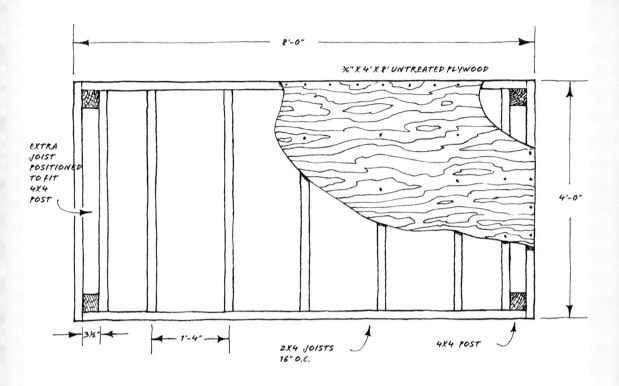

8'-0"

⅜" X 4' X 8' UNTREATED PLYWOOD

4'-0"

EXTRA
JOIST
POSITIONED
TO FIT
4X4
POST

3½"

1'-4"

2X4 JOISTS
16" O.C.

4X4 POST

## CABIN FLOOR

The joist layout of the cabin floor frame includes a 3½-inch space at each end
to capture the top ends of the 4x4 support posts. Bolt the posts to the floor
frame, then add two 2x4 knee braces at each post. A sheet of plywood completes
the floor. If desired, add a custom bench or two between post pairs, as well
as 2x6 shelves adjacent to the hinged wall.

**Base Framing Diagram**

## STAIRS/LADDER

You can build a permanent set of stairs or use a homemade or prefab ladder to reach the cabin. Start with a 48-inch-wide landing anchored to the two front posts and supported with a knee brace on each end. Stair stringers tie into the landing. Precut stringers with eight steps can simplify stair construction.

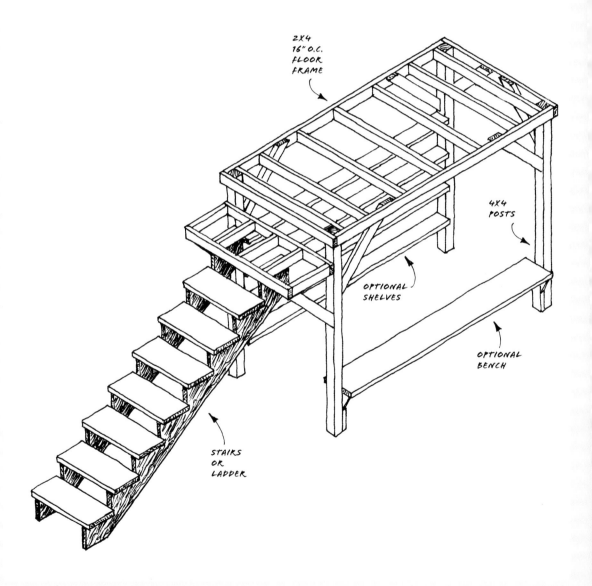

2X4
16" O.C.
FLOOR
FRAME

4X4
POSTS

OPTIONAL
SHELVES

OPTIONAL
BENCH

STAIRS
OR
LADDER

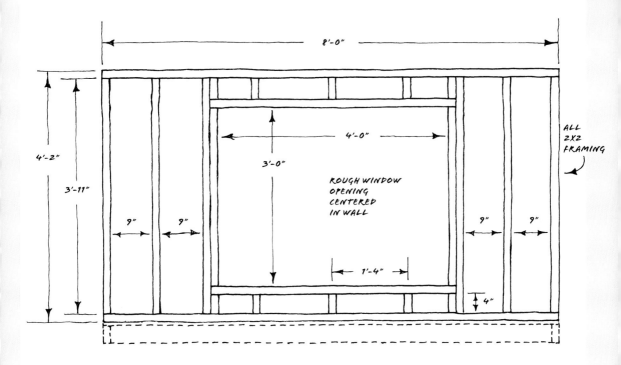

8'-0"

4'-2"

3'-11"

9"

9"

4'-0"

3'-0"

ROUGH WINDOW
OPENING
CENTERED
IN WALL

1'-4"

9"

9"

4"

ALL
2X2
FRAMING

## CABIN WALLS

2x2 wall frames maximize interior space and keep the structure lightweight
(and inexpensive). Modify the window and door openings as needed. The front
and rear walls get 2x4 top plates that form the gable and help support the
roof ridge. The rear wall also gets a 2x4 horizontal plate that serves as a window
header. Cover the outsides of the walls with ½-inch plywood sheathing and
any standard siding, or just plywood siding. The interiors also can be sheathed
and finished, if desired.

**Rear Wall Framing**

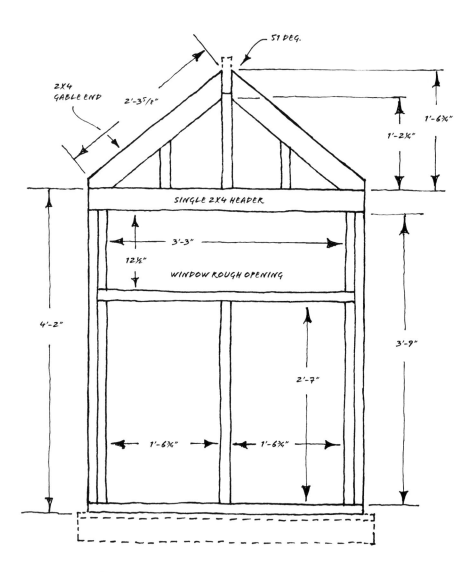

51 DEG.

2X4
GABLE END

2'-3⁵/₈"

1'-6¾"

1'-2¼"

SINGLE 2X4 HEADER

3'-3"

12½"

WINDOW ROUGH OPENING

4'-2"

3'-9"

2'-7"

1'-6¾"    1'-6¾"

2X2 FRAMING EXCEPT WHERE NOTED

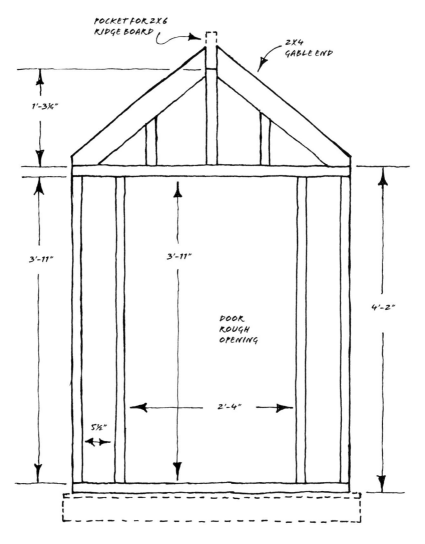

POCKET FOR 2X6
RIDGE BOARD

2X4
GABLE END

1'-3¼"

3'-11"

3'-11"

4'-2"

DOOR
ROUGH
OPENING

2'-4"

5½"

2X2 FRAMING EXCEPT WHERE NOTED

## Roof Framing

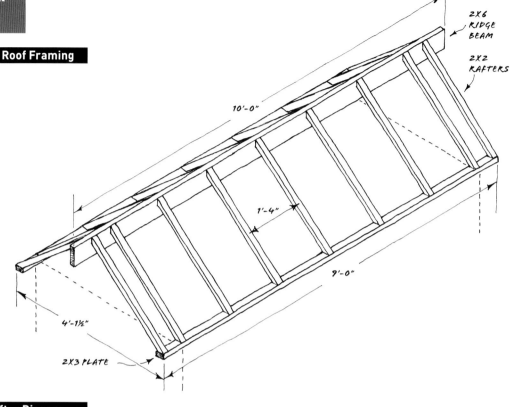

2X6
RIDGE
BEAM

2X2
RAFTERS

10'-0"

1'-4"

9'-0"

4'-1½"

2X3 PLATE

## Rafter Diagrams

2'-6⅞"

51 DEG.

2'-0"

39 DEG.

1'-7⅜"

4'-1½"

## ROOF

The roof frame keeps things light with 2x2 rafters. 2x3s can be used as well. These meet the top of a 2x6 ridge beam that sets into framing pockets on the gable ends. At their bottom ends the rafters rest on 2x3 plates that overhang the outsides of the walls, creating a convenient ledge for butting up the wall sheathing and siding. Sheath the roof with ½-inch plywood. Corrugated polycarbonate roofing (such as Tuftex) works well for both the cabin roof and the covering for the hinged wall.

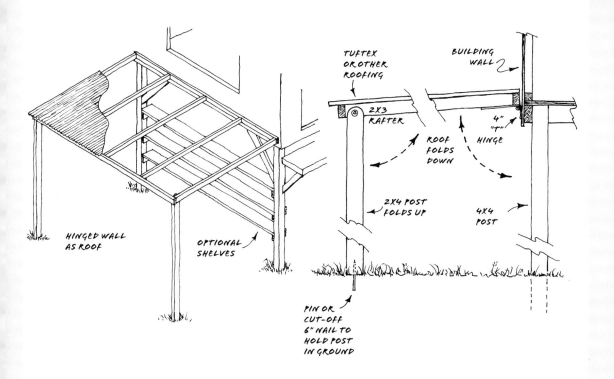

## HINGED WALL

Another lightweight design, the hinged wall is framed with 2x3s and gets three evenly spaced rafters. Top the frame with clear or translucent roofing panels, depending on how much light and heat transmission you want. Mount the wall structure to the cabin base, using heavy-duty exterior hinges anchored into the floor framing. The hinges may need blocks or shims behind to provide clearance for the wall to swing down flush to the 4x4 posts. If desired, flash over the joint with flexible material, such as a strip of flexible rubber or EPDM pond liner.

Add a 2x4 leg to each outside corner of the hinged wall frame, mounting the legs with a single carriage bolt so they can swing up against the wall frame to move it into the *down* position. Add a pin or nail to the bottom ends of the legs (or taper them to a point) so they stick in the ground when the wall is up.

# THE PERMATENT

**M**ATTHEW WOLPE IS COFOUNDER, with partner Kevin McElroy, of the eco-minded building company Just Fine Design/Build, based in Oakland, California. The two have released a book on the tiniest of tiny structures, called *Reinventing the Chicken Coop*, with the approach of making coops as unique, colorful, modern, and aesthetically pleasing as possible. Wolpe is also a senior mechanician in furniture and carpentry at the University of California Berkeley's College of Environmental Design and teaches woodworking at The Crucible, a nonprofit arts school in Oakland. In 2014 he launched the company PRACTICE Community Design/Build. See Matt's creative and gorgeous 100-square-foot house in Oakland on page 16 of this book.

I met Matt when we were both featured speakers at the Yestermorrow Tiny House Fair in 2013 and found him instantly likable and full of great ideas. So I reached out and asked him to design this tiny camp cabin. His design makes great use of outside space by means of a generously overhanging roof, a small deck, and an outdoor kitchen and shower. It even has outdoor storage cabinets, all of which could be fitted with locks. Yes, a cabin like this is best suited for mild climates or seasonal use, but even if that doesn't work for you, it's still full of great ideas that you might borrow.

Here's what the designer says about his building: "As an outpost in a meadow miles from the nearest town, a low-budget country house on a ridge, temporary housing while building a bigger house, or guest accommodations for an urban backyard, the Permatent is just what it sounds like: a permanent tent, inspired by the visual vocabulary of vintage tents and remote national park ranger huts." The structure stands on a 12 x 12-foot deck and, with lightweight framing materials (primarily 2x2s), can be assembled by a single person. It can also be insulated to be weathertight and cozy. Inside, you can add a desk, bed, and storage space. Outside, the side wall conveniently hosts an open-air kitchen and shower.

**96 square feet**

**Matthew Wolpe,
Just Fine Design/
Build**

**Floor Plan**

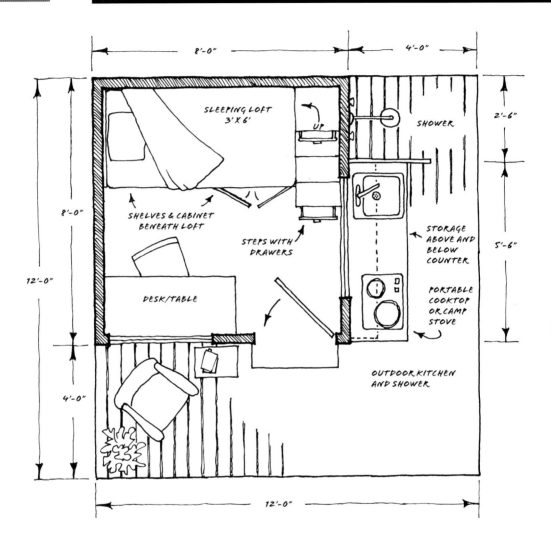

## CONSTRUCTION BASICS

The Permatent combines a simple wood-frame structure with an appealing mix of angles, overhangs, and finish materials that make the design truly distinctive. The roofing, siding, and exterior features play key roles here, and all can be easily modified for custom looks and function.

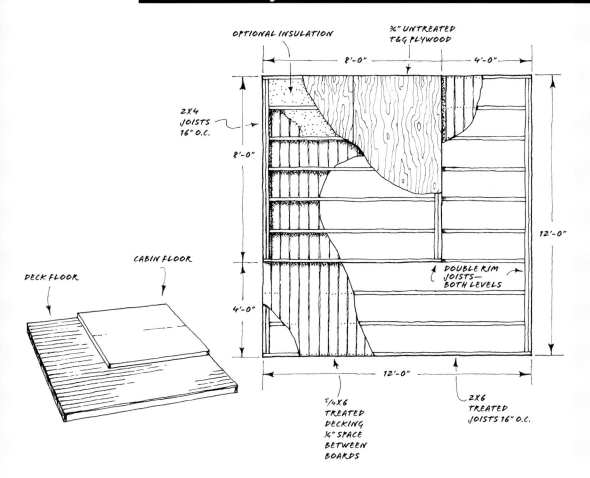

OPTIONAL INSULATION

¾" UNTREATED T&G PLYWOOD

2X4 JOISTS 16" O.C.

8'-0"

4'-0"

8'-0"

12'-0"

CABIN FLOOR

DECK FLOOR

DOUBLE RIM JOISTS— BOTH LEVELS

4'-0"

12'-0"

5/4x6 TREATED DECKING ¼" SPACE BETWEEN BOARDS

2X6 TREATED JOISTS 16" O.C.

## DECK AND CABIN FLOOR

The deck and floor have simple square frames with joists at 16 inches on center and doubled end joists. The deck is treated 2x6s, while the floor is treated 2x4s. Cover the deck with treated ⁵/₄x6 decking boards gapped about ¼ inch for drainage. Sheathe the floor with standard (untreated) ¾-inch plywood.

As an option to save on decking material, you can set the cabin floor frame directly onto the deck frame. If you take this route, you should double the deck joist under the front wall of the cabin to provide support for the decking boards.

## Front Wall

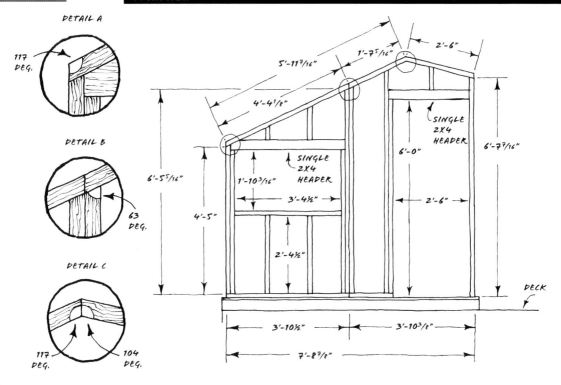

DETAIL A

117 DEG.

DETAIL B

63 DEG.

DETAIL C

117 DEG.          104 DEG.

5'-11⁷/16"

1'-7⁵/16"

2'-6"

4'-4⁷/8"

SINGLE 2X4 HEADER

6'-0"

6'-7⁷/16"

6'-5⁵/16"

SINGLE 2X4 HEADER

1'-10³/16"

3'-4½"

4'-5"

2'-6"

2'-4½"

DECK

3'-10½"          3'-10³/8"

7'-8⁷/8"

## Right Wall

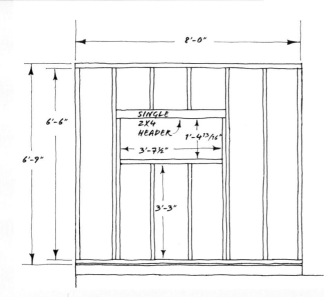

8'-0"

6'-6"

SINGLE 2X4 HEADER

1'-4¹³/16"

3'-7½"

6'-9"

3'-3"

DECK

## WALLS

The four walls are framed with 2x2s and get single-2x4 headers over the windows and door. The front and rear walls can be framed in two sections each, simplifying construction and transport (if necessary). The siding can be plywood or other suitable materials (with sheathing, as needed). If you plan to add cabinets or other wall-mounted fixtures on the right side wall, it's a good idea to sheathe the wall's frame with ¾-inch plywood for backing. Only the front, rear, and right side walls get siding; the left side wall is covered with the roofing material.

## Rear Wall

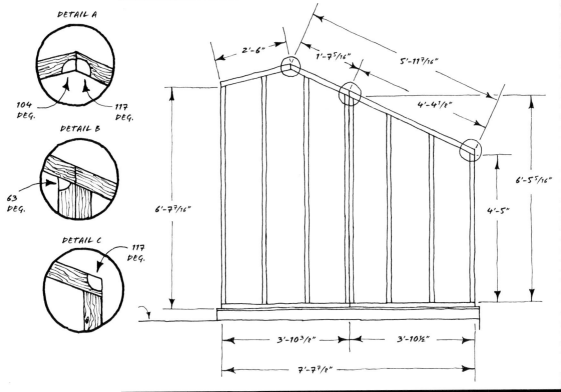

DETAIL A

104 DEG.   117 DEG.

DETAIL B

63 DEG.

DETAIL C   117 DEG.

2'-6"   1'-7⁵/₁₆"   5'-11⁷/₁₆"

4'-4¹/₈"

6'-5⁵/₁₆"

6'-7⁷/₁₆"   4'-5"

3'-10³/₈"   3'-10½"

7'-7⁷/₈"

## Left Wall

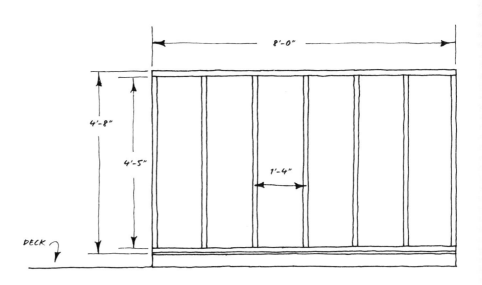

8'-0"

4'-8"

4'-5"

1'-4"

DECK

## Roof Frame and Purlins

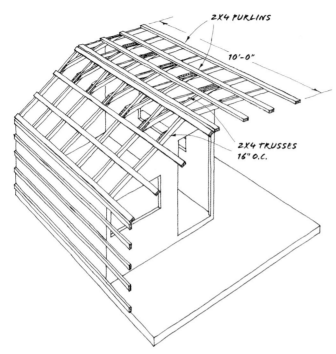

2X4 PURLINS

10'-0"

2X4 TRUSSES
16" O.C.

# ROOF

The roof frame consists of seven trusses made with 2x4s. The five interior trusses get two bottom chords (collar ties) each, while the two end trusses get a single (interior) bottom chord so they can fit onto the front- and rear-wall top plates. Reinforce the joint at the peak of each truss with plywood gussets or metal connector plates.

The roof has no sheathing, so before the corrugated metal (or other) roofing goes on, you need to install 10-foot-long, 2x4 purlins, evenly spaced, along both roof planes, as well as down the left side wall of the cabin. Install the roofing with roofing screws and neoprene washers (or as specified by the manufacturer), making the sure screws won't penetrate the bottom faces of the purlins. Run the roofing a little long on the left side of the roof so it extends beyond the left wall for proper drainage.

## Roof Truss Diagram

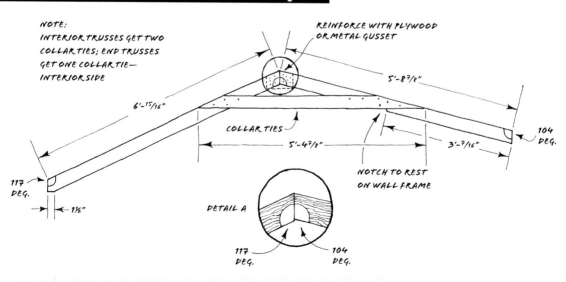

NOTE:
INTERIOR TRUSSES GET TWO
COLLAR TIES; END TRUSSES
GET ONE COLLAR TIE—
INTERIOR SIDE

REINFORCE WITH PLYWOOD
OR METAL GUSSET

5'-8⁷/₁₆"

6'-¹⁵/₁₆"

COLLAR TIES

5'-4⁷/₈"

3'-⁷/₁₆"

104
DEG.

117
DEG.

1½"

NOTCH TO REST
ON WALL FRAME

DETAIL A

117
DEG.

104
DEG.

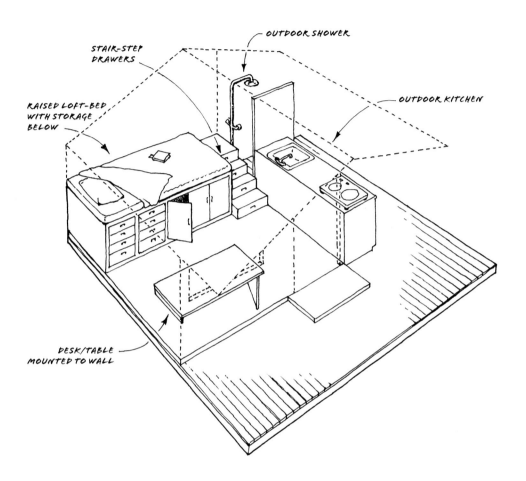

STAIR-STEP
DRAWERS

OUTDOOR SHOWER

RAISED LOFT-BED
WITH STORAGE
BELOW

OUTDOOR KITCHEN

DESK/TABLE
MOUNTED TO WALL

## DOOR AND WINDOWS

With a 30 x 72-inch rough opening, the door is a standard width but short in height. This means you can cut down a solid door or build a custom door to fit. The windows can be salvaged units or custom-made with plastic or glass glazing.

## OPTIONAL BUILT-INS

The designer's plans include some clever ideas for outfitting the cabin interior, including a bed with storage below, a simple wall-hung desk, and storage drawers that form a staircase leading up to the bed.

# THE CAREY CABIN

**32 square feet**

**Deek Diedricksen**

**I**N RECENT YEARS, fledgling Boston-area architect Sean Carey has helped me tremendously a couple of times by rendering many of my already-built cabins, or my sketches, into more readable, functional plan sets. He also did so for the sketches Jay Shafer and I came up with. So while trying to scheme up a funny or bizarre name for this simple little backyard office, I figured, why not just pay tribute and thanks to someone I know? Also, this writer's shack is so small that just a few individuals could "Carey" it from one locale to another. Get it?

The Carey Cabin takes up so little space that it could easily reside on a city rooftop, on an alleylike sliver of land, on the back of a trailer (as small as 4 x 8 feet), or in any backyard or patch of woods. Plus, it's affordable, light, and easy to construct. Because it uses stock-length lumber (or the exact halves of 8-foot lumber runs), full sheets of plywood, and 2x3s instead of 2x4s, this one's not only a friend to your wallet but also to your back. The 2x3s allow for an extra 2 inches of width in the interior, which is more noticeable than you might think. The cabin can be built for only a few hundred dollars. With the exception of the rear window, which likely requires new Plexiglas, the windows can be salvaged, as can many of the building materials.

Aside from being so darn small (but with almost 7 feet of standing room at the peak), this tiny retreat's unusual offering is its deck. The platform can fit a small chair or two and not only adds a little visual depth to the structure, but it also mimics the exact shape of the body and roofline. When not in use, the deck can be flipped up and secured against the cabin's front wall to provide protection during transport or while you're away for long periods.

I imagine the Carey Cabin mainly as a backyard office or writer's retreat. But it could also serve as a tiny shed, a greenhouse (with clear roofing), a meditation room, artist's studio, playhouse, sleep retreat in the woods for two, or outdoor guestroom. And it could easily be tossed onto a platform in a tree.

## CONSTRUCTION BASICS

All of the framing for this tiny structure is joined with screws, and the windows and door need only single-2x3 headers. Custom trim details and finishes can have a big impact on the look of both the exterior and interior. Consider mixing siding materials, and even colors. Shiplap or tongue-and-groove siding on the outside makes for nice ceiling and wall surfaces inside the cabin.

**Framing Diagram**

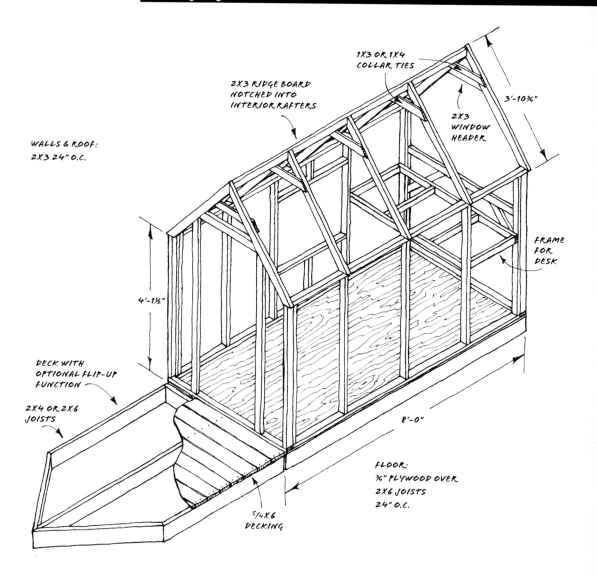

1X3 OR 1X4 COLLAR TIES

2X3 RIDGE BOARD NOTCHED INTO INTERIOR RAFTERS

3'-10¾"

2X3 WINDOW HEADER

WALLS & ROOF: 2X3 24" O.C.

FRAME FOR DESK

4'-1½"

DECK WITH OPTIONAL FLIP-UP FUNCTION

2X4 OR 2X6 JOISTS

8'-0"

5/4X6 DECKING

FLOOR: ¾" PLYWOOD OVER 2X6 JOISTS 24" O.C.

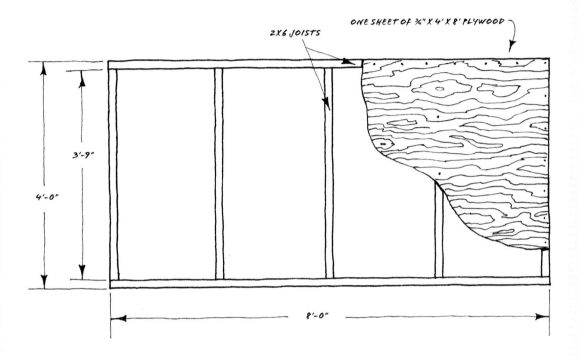

ONE SHEET OF ¾" X 4' X 8' PLYWOOD

2X6 JOISTS

3'-9"

4'-0"

8'-0"

## FLOOR

The floor is a simple platform framed with 2x6s and topped with a full 4 x 8-foot sheet of ¾-inch plywood. You can also frame it with 2x4s if it's evenly supported from below.

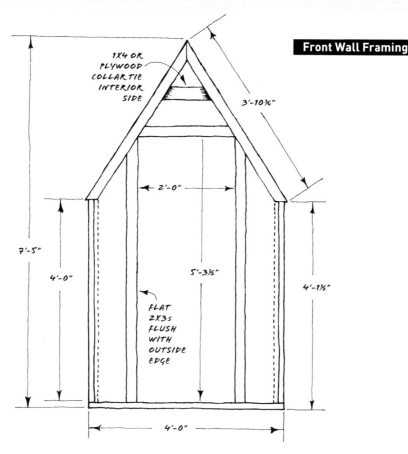

**Front Wall Framing**

1X4 OR PLYWOOD COLLAR TIE INTERIOR SIDE

3'-10⅜"

2'-0"

5'-3½"

FLAT 2X3s FLUSH WITH OUTSIDE EDGE

7'-5"

4'-0"

4'-1½"

4'-0"

## WALLS

Frame the walls with 2x3s and screws. The front and rear walls are the *through* walls and cap over the ends of the side walls. Include the end rafters when framing the front and rear walls (see Roof, below). Each set of end rafters gets a collar tie about 8 inches down from the roof peak. This can be a furring strip, or you can use a triangular plywood gusset for a bit more strength.

On the side walls, place a center stud at the exact center along the length of the wall, then space the intermediate studs evenly at either side. Include rough openings for windows, as desired.

In the project shown, the side walls get ⅜-inch plywood siding. A single 4 x 8-foot sheet running horizontally will cover each side, but the walls are 49½ inches tall, so you have to center the panel up and down so it covers about half of the top and bottom plates equally. Cover the gap along the bottom with trim. The front and rear walls get tongue-and-groove plank siding or other desired material.

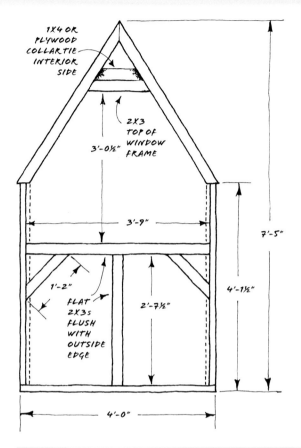

1X4 OR PLYWOOD COLLAR TIE INTERIOR SIDE

2X3 TOP OF WINDOW FRAME

3'-0½"

3'-9"

7'-5"

4'-1½"

1'-2"

FLAT 2X3s FLUSH WITH OUTSIDE EDGE

2'-7½"

4'-0"

## Side Wall Framing

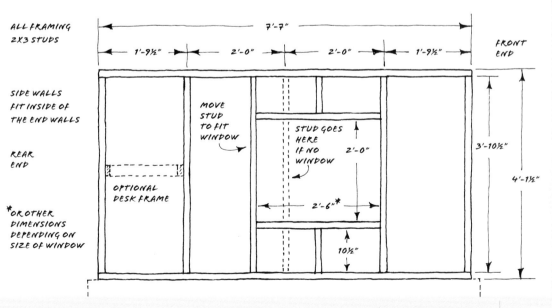

ALL FRAMING 2X3 STUDS

7'-7"

1'-9½"    2'-0"    2'-0"    1'-9½"

FRONT END

SIDE WALLS FIT INSIDE OF THE END WALLS

MOVE STUD TO FIT WINDOW

STUD GOES HERE IF NO WINDOW

2'-0"

3'-10½"

REAR END

4'-1½"

OPTIONAL DESK FRAME

2'-6"*

*OR OTHER DIMENSIONS DEPENDING ON SIZE OF WINDOW

10½"

**Rafter Diagrams**

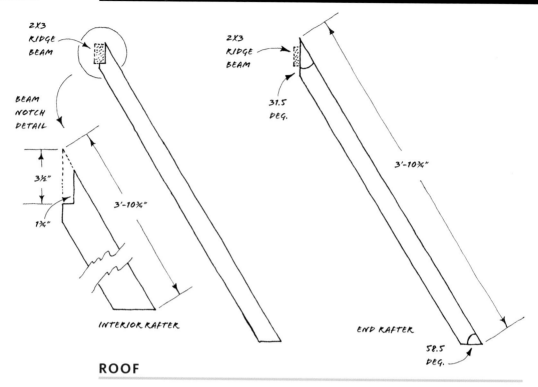

2X3 RIDGE BEAM

BEAM NOTCH DETAIL

3½"

1¾"

3'-10¾"

INTERIOR RAFTER

2X3 RIDGE BEAM

31.5 DEG.

3'-10¾"

END RAFTER

58.5 DEG.

## ROOF

There are two types of rafters: end and interior. The four end rafters are part of the front and rear wall frames. The number of interior rafters is based on the desired spacing; you'll need three sets for approximately 24-inch spacing or five sets for approximately 16-inch spacing.

The ridge beam is a single 2x3. You can leave the ridge with square edges or rip the top edges on a table saw to match the roof slope. In either case, notch the interior rafters to accept the ridge. The two end rafters at each gable do not get notches; the ridge butts into the inside faces of these rafters.

Fasten the top ends of the rafters to the ridge beam by screwing through the outsides of the rafters and into the ridge. Screw the bottom ends of the rafters to the wall plates with one screw driven down through the rafter and into the wall stud or plate, and one opposing screw through the stud or plate and into the rafter. Alternatively, you can use steel framing connectors to fasten the rafters to the walls.

Sheathe the roof with siding planks, plywood, or other material. If your roofing material requires fasteners between rafter locations, make sure the sheathing is thick enough so that the fasteners don't poke through the bottom and into the cabin interior.

## DECK

The shape and finished dimensions of the deck match those of the cabin's end walls. Frame the deck with 2x6s if you'll leave it down permanently, or use 2x4s to build it for the flip-up function. Cover the deck frame with 5/4x6" decking or basic lumber planks. Support the deck from below with custom bench-style platforms or masonry blocks. Anchor the deck to the cabin floor frame with screws or carriage bolts, or mount it to the cabin base with heavy-duty hinges for flip-up action.

## WINDOWS

Plexiglas sheeting works best for the large rear-wall window. Cut the sheet to fit the rough opening, leaving about ¼-inch "float room" on all sides; the glazing should not fit tightly into the opening. Install the glazing with ¾ x ¾-inch stops on both sides, and seal the exterior edges with silicone caulk. Salvaged windows work well for the side walls, especially if you want them to open for ventilation, or you can build custom windows using the same construction as the large rear window.

**Window Details**

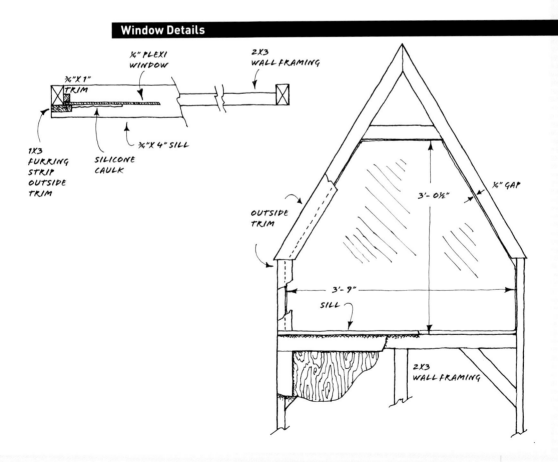

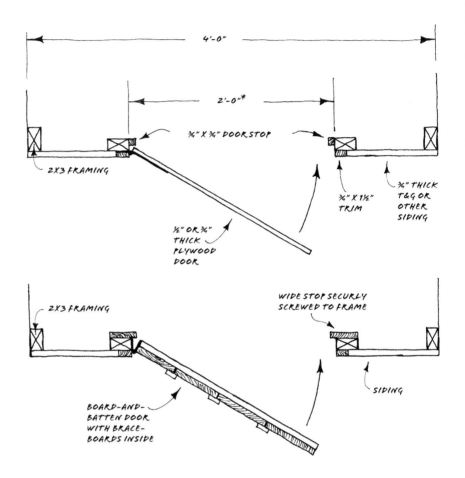

*OR OTHER WIDTH,
BUT A TOO-WIDE
DOOR WILL BE
OUT-OF-SCALE

## DOOR

The door is an easy custom build using good ¾-inch plywood or board-and-batten construction. Size the door based on the actual dimensions of the rough opening, and factor in the hinges, giving the door plenty of clearance in the opening. Hang the door so it opens out, which saves on interior space. Use ¾ x ¾-inch stock for stops wrapping the inside of the opening, or add trim or batten strips to the interior edges of the framing. For a handle, a simple storm door kit with a lock works well.

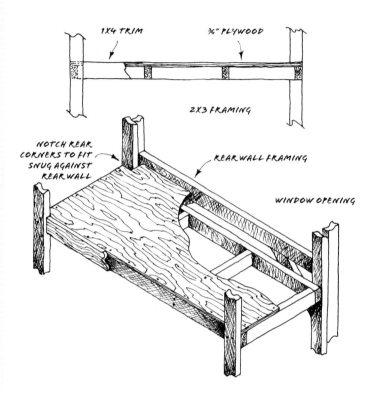

1X4 TRIM

¾" PLYWOOD

2X3 FRAMING

NOTCH REAR CORNERS TO FIT SNUG AGAINST REAR WALL

REAR WALL FRAMING

WINDOW OPENING

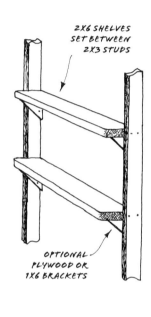

2X6 SHELVES SET BETWEEN 2X3 STUDS

OPTIONAL PLYWOOD OR 1X6 BRACKETS

## BUILT-INS

Construct a simple built-in desk under the large rear window with 2x3 framing topped with plywood leftover from the door (if applicable). Add a piece of trim along the front to cover the plywood edge and framing lumber. Built-in shelves take advantage of framing cavities; build these with 2x6 or 2x4 planks cut to fit between two wall studs. It's a good idea to round off the exposed corners of the shelves to prevent boo-boos. Screw through the outsides of the studs and into the edges of the shelf planks.

# THE WOODSY WAGGON

**32 square feet**

**Sage Rad**

**A** BUILDER AND DESIGNER, CARPENTER BY TRADE, partially off-grid homesteader, beekeeper, and tiny-house (well, gypsy wagon) dweller, Sage Rad is one interesting and passionate dude, and he's constantly working on one project or another. I shared his preliminary designs for this cute 'n' cozy little dwelling on wheels on my blog. Its simple approach and good looks made an impression on me, and I later asked Sage to share the final design. I'm hoping that someday we might see a vast array of creative takes on this fun, affordable little structure.

"I just want to build one of these, leave the city, roll it into the woods somewhere, and live out of it," Sage told me. This is coming from a guy who now lives in a self-built, salvaged-material gypsy wagon on the outskirts of Boston, and who once ditched college to live in a tree house in the middle of the Massachusetts woods. So I tend to believe him.

The Woodsy Waggon gets its name from traditional gypsy "waggons" of old Europe, and it's designed to be a smaller version of the same: a pullable, lightweight wagon with a small sleep space, counter space for food prep, and storage. It also has a hinged stoop/seat over the front handlebars, which makes a great campfire seat and can flip up to help secure the cabin door.

## CONSTRUCTION BASICS

All portable structures require careful consideration of the trade-off between strength and weight. When building the Waggon, you can opt for thicker plywood for stiffer, stronger walls, floor, and door, or go for lightness with thinner material. If your aim is to be as light as possible, use lightweight lumber (or other material) for braces and supports to stiffen panels or strengthen corner joints as needed. Just keep in mind the extra weight of the bracing to make sure the trade-off is worth it.

**Base**

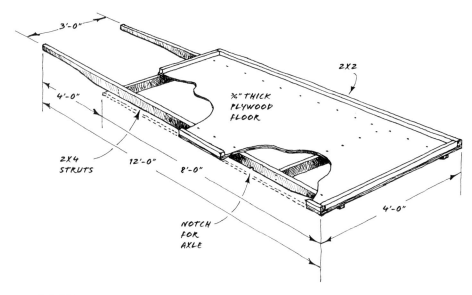

## BASE

As a wheeled structure, the Waggon has a base that's part chassis and part cabin floor. It starts with two 12-foot-long 2x4 struts joined with two or more 2x4 cross braces (or joists). The struts are shaped into handles at one end, while the other ends get a simple taper. This chassis frame gets topped with a full 4 x 8-foot sheet of plywood. You can use ½-inch or ¾-inch, but you might want an extra cross brace or two with thinner material. Glue and screw 2x2s along the perimeter on the top face of the plywood. This stiffens the floor and provides backing for fastening the plywood walls. Notch the struts to accept an axle for the wheels, or use whatever system your project requires. For the wheels you can use anything that rolls and is strong enough to support the Waggon and its occupant(s).

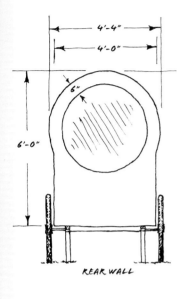

REAR WALL

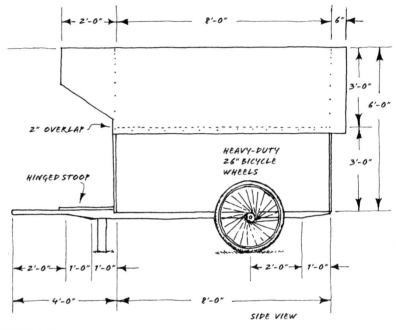

2" OVERLAP

HINGED STOOP

HEAVY-DUTY
26" BICYCLE
WHEELS

SIDE VIEW

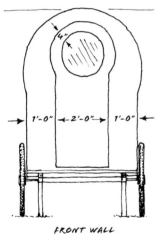

FRONT WALL

## WALLS

The plywood walls can be as thin as $\frac{3}{8}$ inch and as thick as $\frac{3}{4}$ inch. Fasten the walls to the outsides of the 2x2s on the base, and join the wall panels at each corner with a vertical 2x2 on the cabin interior. The front and rear walls cover the edges of the side walls, and all cover the edges of the base plywood.

## WINDOWS

Use Plexiglas for the windows in the rear wall and the door. The windows can be any size and shape you like. Just make sure there's enough wood around the glazing for strength. You can set the glazing into a rabbeted edge in the plywood and secure it with caulk, or cut the Plexiglas 2 inches or so larger than the opening and screw it to the interior side of the plywood. A screened ventilation panel, or a small window that opens, might also be a good idea.

## DOOR

Hang the door so it opens out, using stops on the inside of the opening to prevent the door from swinging in. Choose the best handle/latch and lock for your needs. A simple screen door handle kit might do the trick, or add something more heavy-duty for security.

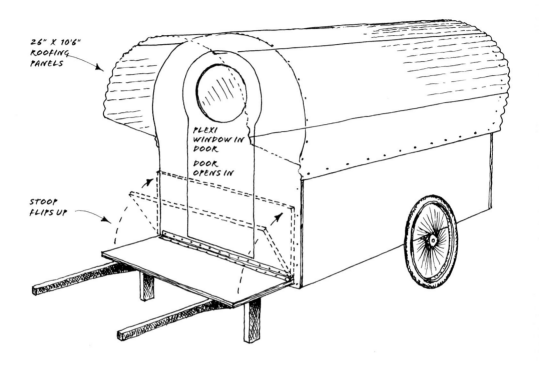

26" X 10'6"
ROOFING
PANELS

PLEXI
WINDOW IN
DOOR

DOOR
OPENS IN

STOOP
FLIPS UP

## ROOF

The barrel-shaped roof is made with Tuftex (or similar) polycarbonate roofing panels fastened to the walls with roofing screws with neoprene washers. Secure the panels to the faces of the side walls and to the edges of the front and rear walls (or screw into lightweight blocking if the plywood is too thin). If any sag occurs in the middle of the roof, you might want to jigsaw-cut a side-to-side arched rafter from plywood (that matches the front and rear roof curve) to further support the polycarbonate.

## FRONT STOOP

The front stoop doubles as a handy bench seat and can be flipped up on hinges to cover the lower portion of the door, where you can secure it with some latches and locks, if desired. You can make the stoop with plywood (¾-inch, or two layers of ⅜- or ½-inch if you have scraps) or build a small frame and top it with four $5/4 \times 6$ decking planks gapped about ¼ inch apart.

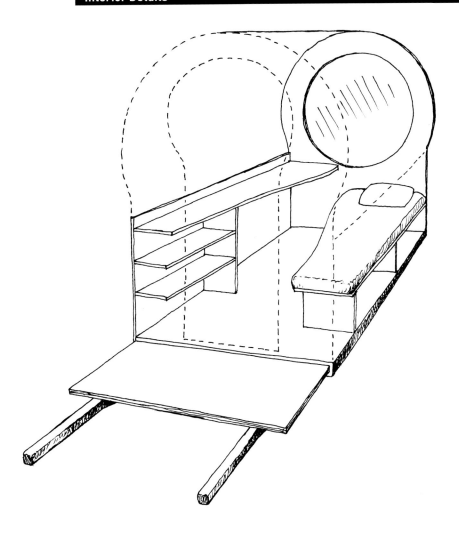

## OPTIONAL BUILT-INS

A platform bed and full-length table or shelf take advantage of the long cabin
space. Both can be made with plywood, secured to the walls with cleats,
and supported with vertical posts. Hang the bed platform from the cleats with
hinges, if you desire, for a flip-up/flip-down bed. Add smaller shelves below
the table using simple brackets.

# RESOURCES

More of Deek Diedricksen's work can be found at www.relaxshacks.com.

**ALEX PINO**
tinyhousetalk
tinyhousetalk.com

**ANDREW ODOM**
Tiny r(E)volution
tinyrevolution.us

**ANGELA RAMSEYER**
mightymicrobuilt.com
The Mighty Micro House, p.138

**BLUE MOON RISING**
bluemoonrising.org
The Luna Bleu, p.44

**BONEYARD STUDIOS**
boneyardstudios.org
The Matchbox, p.46

**CHRIS & MALISSA TACK**
The Tiny Tack House
chrisandmalissa.com

**CHRISTOPHER SMITH &
MERETE MUELLER**
TINY
tiny-themovie.com

**DAN LOUCHE**
Tiny House Builder
tinyhousebuilder.com

**DAVE FRAZEE**
Broken Arrow Workshop
brokenarrowworkshop.com
The Miner's Shelter, p.77

**ELLA JENKINS**
littleyellowdoor
littleyellowdoor.wordpress.com
Little Yellow, p.18

**GEOFF BAKER**
Westcoast Outbuildings
outbuildings.ca

**THE GNOMADIK
WORKSHOP**
gnomadik.com
The Gnomadik, p.135

**GUILLAUME DUTILH**
Tiny House Giant Journey
tinyhousegiantjourney.com
The Giant Journey Home, p.51

**HELLE KVAMME**
hellekvamme.se
The Steam Studio, p.114

**HINTERLAND**
hinterlanddesign.com
The Hinterland Studio, p.82

**HOBBITAT**
hobbitatspaces.com
The Luna Bleu, p.44

**HOLLY GOMEZ**
A Place Imagined
aplaceimagined.com
The Micro Dogtrot Cabin, p.212

**JAMAICA COTTAGE SHOP**
jamaicacottageshop.com
The Writer's Haven, p.65

**JAY SHAFER**
Four Lights Tiny House
fourlightshouses.com
The Stilted Sleeper, p.222

**JOE COOVER**
Long Story Short House
longstoryshorthouse.com

**JOEL HENRIQUES**
made by joel
madebyjoel.com
The Little Orange Playhouse,
p.150

**JOSEPH EBSWORTH**
Solar Burrito Blog
solarburrito.com

**JUST FINE DESIGN/BUILD**
justfinedesignbuild.com
Matt Wolpe's Tiny House, p.16

**KENT GRISWOLD**
Tiny House Blog
tinyhouseblog.com

**MACY MILLER**
MiniMotives
minimotives.com

**MICHAEL JANZEN**
Tiny House Design
tinyhousedesign.com

**MODFRUGAL**
modfrugal.com
The ModFruGal Stilt House,
p.120

**MORTEN NISKER
TOPPENBERG**
nisker.net
The Nisker Nook, p.154

**NELSON TINY HOUSES**
nelsontinyhouses.com
The V House, p.48

**OIXIO ARTS**
oixio.com
The Pico-Dwelling, p.34

**PEPPER CLARK**
Bungalow to Go
bungalowtogo.com

**PLANKBRIDGE LTD.**
plankbridge.com
Shepherd's Huts, p.130

**SLEEPBOX**
sleepbox.co.uk
Sleepbox, p.96

**STEVEN HARRELL**
Tiny House Listings
tinyhouselistings.com
Tiny House Swoon
tinyhouseswoon.com

**TENNESSEE TINY HOMES**
tennesseetinyhomes.com
Mendy's Shoe Box, p.25

**TUMBLEWEED TINY
HOUSE COMPANY**
tumbleweedhouses.com
The Tumbleweed Linden, p.28;
Little Yellow, p.18; The Giant
Journey Home, p. 51

**WILL YOUNT**
Hummingbird Tiny Spaces
hummingbirdtinyspaces.com
The Sawtooth, p.204

**YESTERMORROW DESIGN/
BUILD SCHOOL**
yestermorrow.org
The 227, p.22

---

## PHOTOGRAPHY CREDITS

© 2012 Matt Glass and Jordan Long, courtesy of Nick Olson and Lilah Horwitz, designer/builders: 3 (top left), 6 (top), 91, 92

© 2013 Andrew Prince: 69, 70 (bottom)

© Andrew Pogue Photography: 34–36, 40–42, 187 (left), (second from bottom)

© Angela Ramseyer/MightyMicroBuilt.com: 138, 139

© Bjon Pankratz: 124, 125

© Brittany M. Powell: 16, 17

© Bruce Damer, Ancient Oaks Farm: 8, 71, 72

Courtesy of Jesse Selman: 22 (top)

Courtesy of Sleepbox, Ltd.: 96, 97

© Dave Frazee: 78 (middle)

© Dawn and Ella Jenkins: 18–20

© Derek Diedricksen: 1, 3 (top right), 6 (middle), 7, 9 (top), 10, 22 (bottom left and right), 23, 24, 37–39, 44 (top), 46, 47, 58–64, 70 (top), 75, 79–81, 86–89, 94, 98, 99 (bottom), 106–108, 112, 113, 116–119, 122, 123, 126, 127, 133, 134, 142, 143, 150–153, 156–159, 162, 174, 177, 178, 180, 182, 183 (all except bottom), 185, 186, 187 (except left, second from bottom), 190, 193–199, 202

© Dianne Sedore-McCoy: 67, 68

© Dustin Diedricksen: 99 (top)

© Garner O. Boyd – Photographer: 25–27

© Guillaume Dutilh @ Tiny House Giant Journey: 51, 53

© Helle Kvamme: 114, 115

© henryn0580/iStockphoto.com: 183 (bottom)

© jamaicacottageshop.com: 65, 66

© Jean-Marc and Maggie Labrosse: 146, 147

© Jennifer Yee: 31–33

© John Polak: 5, 73, 74, 90, 95, 140, 141

© Karlo Gesner: 44 (bottom), 45

© Katherine Dekker: 93

© Mimi Day: 144–145

© ModFruGal: 6 bottom, 120, 121

© Morten Nisker Toppenberg: 154, 155

© Nathan Rist: 3 bottom, 76, 77, 78 (top right and bottom)

© Palo Coleman: 9 (bottom)

© Richard Lee: 130–132

© Riley McFerrin: 82, 83

© Sean F. White: 3 (middle), 135–137

© Sebastien Barre/http://barre.me: 109–111

© Seth Reidy: 48–50

© Suzy Wimbourne Photography: 56, 57

© Swen Rudolph Photographer // Berlin: 78 (top left)

© Tim Klein: 2, 104, 105

© Tumbleweed Tiny House Co.: 28–30

© Tyler Rodgers: 84, 85

© Will White: 100, 101